How To Play Golf

SAM SNEAD'S

How To Play Golf

AND PROFESSIONAL TIPS ON
IMPROVING YOUR SCORE

ALSO

Special Section

BY THE UNIVERSITY OF MICHIGAN'S
FAMOUS GOLF COACH,
BERT KATZENMEYER

GARDEN CITY BOOKS

Garden City, New York

One of golf's most popular figures, "Slamming" Sam Snead, has just completed a decade under the big top. According to golf's foremost authorities, he is one of the finest "natural" golfers who have appeared in generations. It was under a Hot Springs, Va., dateline, September 20, 1935, that the following appeared in the newspapers of the country:

"Sam Snead, young local assistant pro making his debut in major competition, rocked par with a 68 this morning, then skidded downhill for a dozen holes, only to rally along the second-round stretch for a 76 and 144 total that brought him a three-shot lead in the $2,500 Cascades seventy-two hole open golf championship."

That paragraph blazed the trail of one of golf's most brilliant and entertaining luminaries. Snead's rise to fame was meteoric indeed. By 1938 he was top money winner and was proclaimed the year's outstanding golfer and presented with the award emblematic of that distinction in the Court of Sport at the New York World's Fair. The presentation was made by George Jacobus, then president of the Professional Golfers' Association of America. The "honor guard" comprised such outstanding pros as Horton Smith, Byron Nelson, Ed Dudley, Leo Diegel and Dick Metz.

Snead dropped to sixth in the winter tour of 1939-40. He had embarked upon that tour under a psychological handicap for it was in June of 1939 that he had taken that disastrous 8 on the last hole of the seventy-two which had lost him the national open championship. The following year Snead had another disappointment when he was defeated by Byron Nelson in the final of the national P.G.A. at Hershey by the margin of one hole. Coming back to win that honor in 1942, his first national success, Snead found himself within a few days of entering the United States Navy. For two years Sam was out of competition but his come back was sensational.

Beginning the comeback at Portland where he was first with a score of 289 in the late winter of 1944 Snead tied for third at San Francisco, tied for seventh at Oakland, was first at Richmond with 278 and ushered in the season of 1945 by leading the field at Los Angeles. Later he won at Gulfport after a double tie with Nelson.

On top of this Snead captured the tournaments at Pensacola and Jacksonville, the latter marking his third straight medal-play victory. At Jacksonville he scored 266, which was 22 under par. Snead was in the semi-finals of the Miami four-ball matches and in the next medal play event, that at Charlotte, again tied with Nelson but this time lost on a double play off.

From Portland to Atlanta, in eighteen tournaments, Snead won $16,861. A broken wrist cost him dearly during most of the summer tournaments but he had caught up with the pack again by the time he reached Dallas in September, winning there by four strokes from a field that included Nelson, Hogan and McSpaden.

Samuel Jackson Snead's whiplash swing stands in the forefront of all for gallery appeal. In its flowing smoothness its power may be deceiving. Nevertheless it is the kind of swing the ordinary golfer seems to understand and most desires to cultivate. By staying in the top class he has demonstrated that his game is basically sound.

Fore!

THE FOLLOWING LESSONS are written in simple language so that the player can easily understand them, apply them to his individual swing, and quickly correct minor faults that may have developed.

They will aid the beginner in getting a clear idea of how the swing should be made, and will state reasons why certain fundamentals are adhered to, and what can be expected if they are not.

They are not written with the intention of making a champion out of all who read them, or with the idea that the golfer need not seek further instruction.

The answers to nearly all questions concerning the swing will be found in the following articles. By following their instructions, the player will more quickly grasp the ideas a professional instructor tries to convey, thus hastening progress in developing his game.

Contents

The Value of Instruction

IT IS TRUE that a player can bring his score down to what is considered good golf without instruction, but he never will be able fully to enjoy the game until he has developed a certain amount of consistency. The beginner should never go near a golf course until he has some idea as to how the ball should be hit.

The player who attempts to learn the game without instruction forms incorrect habits which are a handicap to satisfactory headway. This type of golfer prides himself on the fact that he is self-taught, little realizing that he is falling into errors that will be hard to correct when, and if, he has to see a competent instructor.

Such a golfer will improve to a certain degree, there is no doubt, but never will he be of championship caliber, and soon he will reach a stage where improvement ceases. Without a thorough knowledge of the fundamentals, he cannot achieve a high degree of efficiency.

It is an inconsiderable percentage of golfers who ever succeed in getting down to a point where they are scratch players.

Without a good instructor, golf looks easy to the beginner, and he thinks he can learn the game unaided. He fails to realize that to err is human, and that it is natural to do incorrectly the movements that are required to swing the club successfully.

To teach people how to play the game of golf as well as possible is my job — and that of all professionals — but since there are golfers who do not have the time or the means to obtain individual instruction I will try to present, in as few words as possible, the fundamentals of golf, and will try to impress upon the golfer the simplest reasons why this or that should be done to acquire a stroke that will give the player a certain degree of satisfaction, and start him on the correct path.

Your teacher, including myself, will get as much satisfaction out of knowing that we have helped you break a hundred or have brought your score down to an all-time low, as if we were doing it ourselves for the first time. Instruction is expendable if the player desires to get his game down to a point where he can give par or the best player in the club a good tussle.

Remember, when visiting your pro, each individual has certain peculiarities. His form is as personal as his handwriting. It is his alone.

Since all golfers are not built alike, they do not swing alike, and it is impossible to use the same standard methods to teach the short player that would be used to perfect a good swing in the taller player. The teacher can make alterations in the swing, to fit the individual style, without wandering from the basic fundamentals.

The pupil is the one who has the necessary mental and physical parts for the golf stroke, but it is only the good instructor who can assemble them so that they fit properly, are in relation to each other, are timed, and are in perfect harmony.

If there is any departure from the correct method of bringing the clubhead into the ball at the right angle, the golf instructor is capable of analyzing the cause and effect. Having made instruction of the Royal and Ancient game a profession and his business, the pro is well equipped with a sound knowledge and understanding of his subject. He is an expert in his field. You will soon note through association with your instructor that he is able to catalogue various causes for misplayed shots. For example, there is more than one reason why a shot is sliced. Each is caused by a variation from the correct method, be it a failure to keep the left arm straight, or an overpowering of the left side by the right. The pro readily can see and detect which fault is causing the clubhead to meet the ball inaccurately. After he has made the correction, the player then can practice, and be sure that he is not molding a bad habit by a continuous execution of the fault, hoping that the old feeling of good stroking will soon return of its own accord.

Tutorage under a competent instructor is worth much more than the slight remuneration you will pay him. You not only will be shown the correct method of swinging, but your stroke will be under constant scrutiny. This will keep your stroke in a constant groove, and your instructor will be able quickly to check a wrong before it becomes a habit.

It is my recommendation that the person who has never played golf first acquire, through a professional or through study and practice, a fair knowledge of the fundamentals of the swing. The game of golf is not just a case of hitting the ball around a pasture. It is scientific and it is based on proven facts and fundamentals. Teaching the beginner is easier for the professional than teaching a golfer who has played some. The novice has not as yet formed opinions of his own, nor has he started to construct an incorrect swing that must be torn down and rebuilt. The beginner heeds the advice of the pro, puts it to good use, and develops rapidly. It is hard to correct the player who has a slight knowledge of what the stroke is composed. This player has his own ideas and explanations for what he thinks is causing the trouble. It is hard to convince him that he is at fault. This player, perhaps, has taken lessons from more than one professional without giving any instructor a fair chance to do him any good. A golf lesson can only help if the player will practice what he is told and shown until it becomes a natural thing for him to do without requiring a great deal of thought.

See your professional at your earliest convenience so that you do not fall into the category of the player who is hardest of all to teach. He is the one that is always experimenting with his game, changing his grip and swing. Once established and approved by your instructor, you should never change your grip or any part of it that would alter your natural swing. A good knowledge of the fundamentals requires no changes that will throw your whole game out of alignment.

Your pro will teach you the fundamentals, get them firmly set in your mind, and, with intelligent practice, the swing will soon become automatic. It is then grooved.

The professional, aside from being your teacher, has your interests at heart. He wants to see you enjoy the game, play it to the best of your ability, and furnish you with the proper equipment to accomplish the best results. He is invaluable in aiding you in the selection of the proper playing equipment, and will keep you posted on the latest design and developments of clubs, balls, and wearing apparel. He will listen to your lamentations — why the putt didn't drop on the eighteenth, or why you hooked in the rough on the eleventh. He will be your father confessor of golf. Take your golf troubles to him.

Selection of Golf Equipment

A WORKMAN IS NO BETTER THAN HIS TOOLS, and it is a poor golfer who blames his, providing he has good equipment. Of course, if his clubs are outmoded, he then has fair grounds to blame his tools.

Proof that improvement in golfing equipment has improved the game itself, is to be had in the records of the National Open. Fred Herd, in 1898, won this classic with a score of 328. Ralph Guldahl, in 1937 at Oakland Hills, Birmingham, Michigan, registered 281, paring 47 strokes from Herd's mark. This was made possible only through improvement in equipment.

It has been a far step from the old gutta percha to the modern liquid center and tightly-wound ball. Modern methods have brought all manufacture to such a high standard that what was considered the tops ten years ago, is now outdated and obsolete. So it is in golf.

In the days of the individual club-maker, the design and the workmanship that went into a club was good. These gentlemen were artists at their trade. But where they could turn out one masterpiece, it was difficult, if not humanly impossible, to duplicate the stick once it was broken or discarded for other reasons. They could not fit a brassie or a spoon to a driver, so that each of the clubs would be in relation to one another, and would have the same feel.

Before the event of matched clubs, it was necessary to be a curio collector. The player selected one club from here and another from there until he had a set that was in close harmony. He sometimes spent a lifetime doing this, and still never achieved his goal.

Today, clubs are made to precision. Manufacturers make thousands of them that look alike, feel alike, have the same whippiness in the shafts, and are counter parts in other details — much in the same manner as the automobile manufacturer turns out automobiles of the same design. Matched sets are harmonized so that the feel of the No. 9 iron is the same as the No. 2 iron in relation to weight, length, and balance. Differently weighted or unbalanced clubs require different timing, but if they are of the same family, the swing for each is much the same.

If you are in the market for a set of clubs, it is best to consult your professional or a reliable store. Clubs must be fitted to the individual, much in the same manner as is a suit of clothes. The professional can advise you as to the proper length of shaft, and also the proper lie of the clubhead. If the shaft is not of the right length, the lie will be wrong. If the club is too short, the golfer then has to bend over too far in reaching the ball, and takes a position at address that is unnatural and uncomfortable. If the club is too long, the swinging arc is flattened, and greater accuracy is necessary to have the clubhead meet the ball at the correct angle. To be sure that you are properly fitted, the professional will have you take a natural stance and then note whether the clubhead lies flat or whether it is resting on its toe or heel. Many bad shots are caused by clubs turning in the player's hands as the toe or heel hits the ground.

Remember, the professional is as anxious as the golfer to fit clubs properly, for it gives the player confidence, and progress in developing a good swing is more rapidly achieved. The professional knows that a light club can be swung faster than a heavy one, and that if the club is too light, the player will exert extra effort in attempting to assist the club in doing its work. Alterations can be made by adding weight to the clubhead, but if the club is too heavy, the golfer will feel that the clubhead is dragging and, to speed it up, start hitting too soon. The important thing is to see that the swinging weight of the club is balanced, and that the club is properly weighted for the individual swing.

These reasons should show a golfer the value of good equipment. But there are still other reasons. The modern driver should have enough loft and a deep face, not like those of a decade ago that were shallow, requiring the ball to be teed close to the ground. The player will gain confidence with this type of club as he can tee the ball higher, and this will give him the feeling that it is impossible for him to miss the ball. On the other hand, the brassie and the spoon will, and should, have a shallower face and more loft to be able to fit snugly against the ball lying on the fairway. The grips should be such that they fit the hands, tapering near the end so that the left hand will have the feeling of firmer gripping.

Depending on the player's swing, the shafts selected should be stiff or whippy. If one is a rapid swinger with considerable wrist action who hits the ball hard, stiff shafts are advisable. But if one is a slow swinger, more action will be put into the clubhead by a shaft that is flexible. The older player will benefit by having his clubs fitted with a whippy shaft. He will find the club doing more of the work, fatigue will be lessened, and the round will not require the physical stamina that it has in the past.

Proper attire is almost as important to good golf as proper equipment. Experience has taught the golfer that freedom of legs and arms, and a free turn of the torso are essential to proper swinging. One must be comfortable to execute correctly the movements of the golf swing. Shots call for concentration, so if the golfer is properly attired, he need not worry about this or that being out of place, which is bound to distract his mind from the shot. Designers have noted that clothes for golf should be loose fitting, and have added pleats here and there so that the player will be comfortable, and thus be enabled to get freedom in the swing.

In a book by Glenna Collett Vare, she tells of the woman who was playing a match wearing a knitted dress. In those days, women were wearing dresses quite a few inches longer than today. A terrific storm blew up, soaking this woman to the skin, and causing the dress to sag until it was trailing on the ground. Her morale was upset, and the self-assurance that the well-dressed woman has, was lost. This resulted in her losing the match despite having been several holes ahead.

Today a player can obtain weather-proof clothing, not only jackets, but trousers and wrap-around skirts as well. The golfers that play a lot should have these accessories strapped to their bag.

Shoes are an important item. They should fit well and by all means should have spikes. It is impossible correctly to execute the stroke when the feet are not well anchored and the player is continually thinking and worrying about his feet.

Importance of Proper Grip

Importance of Proper Grip

THE HANDS are the key station transmitting power from the body to the club. The grip is the connection in this central office that must be sound, for a faulty connection cannot transmit the impulses of the body, no matter how good they may be. Therefore, the grip is the all-important fundamental of the stroke. In it the final control of the club rests.

Proper gripping is essential if the clubhead is to meet the ball squarely. The hands must not be turned over to the left so far that the face of the clubhead strikes the ball while it is in an open position; neither should the hands be turned over too far to the right so that a rolling action of the hands at impact hoods the club. They should be placed in relation to the shaft so that in working together, providing the action of the body is correct, they will bring the clubhead into the ball at right angles to the desired line of flight.

We will assume that the proper grip is that which has been generally adopted by the better class of players. It was first molded by Harry Vardon, and bears his name. It is also called the overlapping grip. Vardon placed his left hand on the club so that a "V," formed by the index finger and the thumb of the left hand, pointed over the right shoulder. This brings the left hand in a position to offer a restraining resistance to the right hand that is constantly trying to overpower it. It also gives the golfer a firmer grip with the fingers than when the club is gripped by the palm of the hand.

The right hand is placed so that it will be free to exert extra effort when called on to whip the clubhead through the ball. It is not too far under the shaft so that a wrist snap is halted, but in a position in which, were the palm of the hand open, it would be presented to the hole, or in a plane at right angles to the intended line of flight. The "V" formed by the index finger and the thumb should also point over the right shoulder.

Since the hands should work in unison, they should be united either by an overlapping of the index finger of the left hand by the little finger of the right, or by interlocking the two fingers.

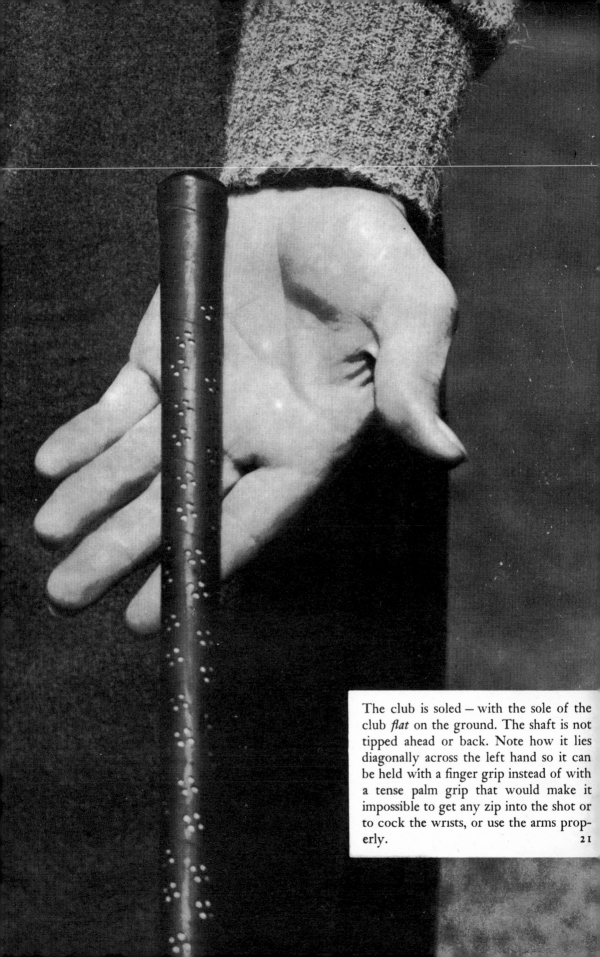

The club is soled — with the sole of the club *flat* on the ground. The shaft is not tipped ahead or back. Note how it lies diagonally across the left hand so it can be held with a finger grip instead of with a tense palm grip that would make it impossible to get any zip into the shot or to cock the wrists, or use the arms properly.

21

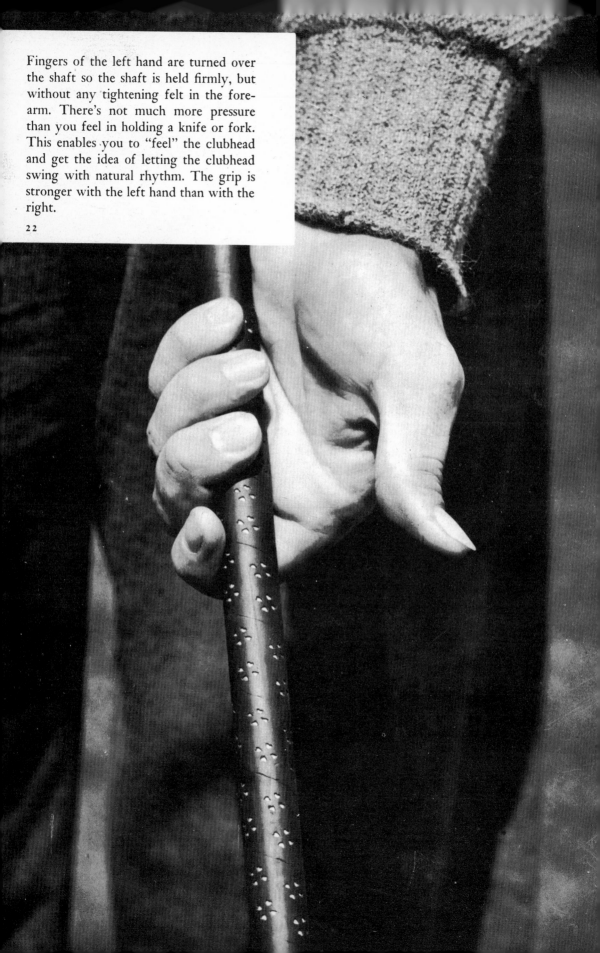

Fingers of the left hand are turned over the shaft so the shaft is held firmly, but without any tightening felt in the forearm. There's not much more pressure than you feel in holding a knife or fork. This enables you to "feel" the clubhead and get the idea of letting the clubhead swing with natural rhythm. The grip is stronger with the left hand than with the right.

22

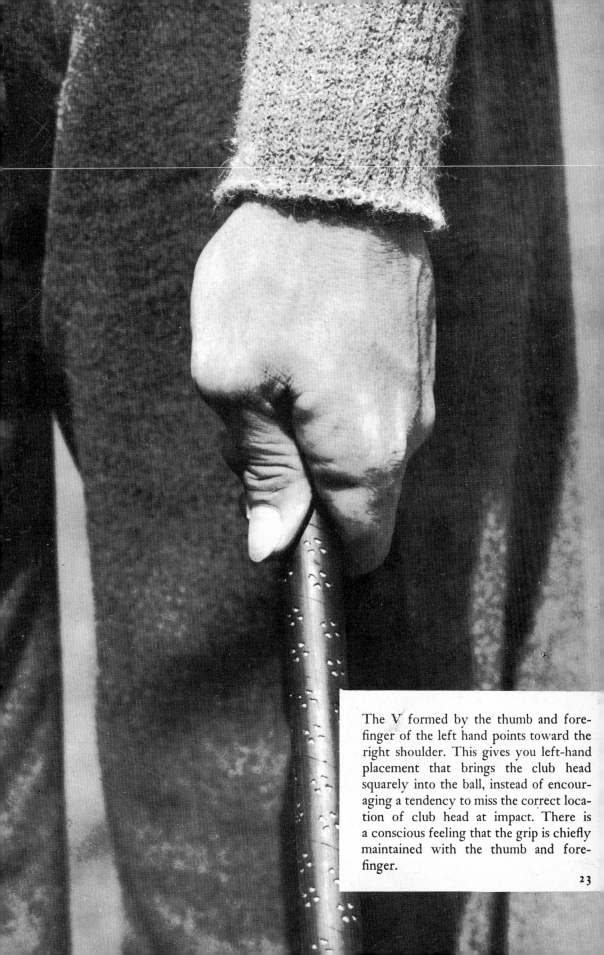

The V formed by the thumb and fore-finger of the left hand points toward the right shoulder. This gives you left-hand placement that brings the club head squarely into the ball, instead of encouraging a tendency to miss the correct location of club head at impact. There is a conscious feeling that the grip is chiefly maintained with the thumb and fore-finger.

23

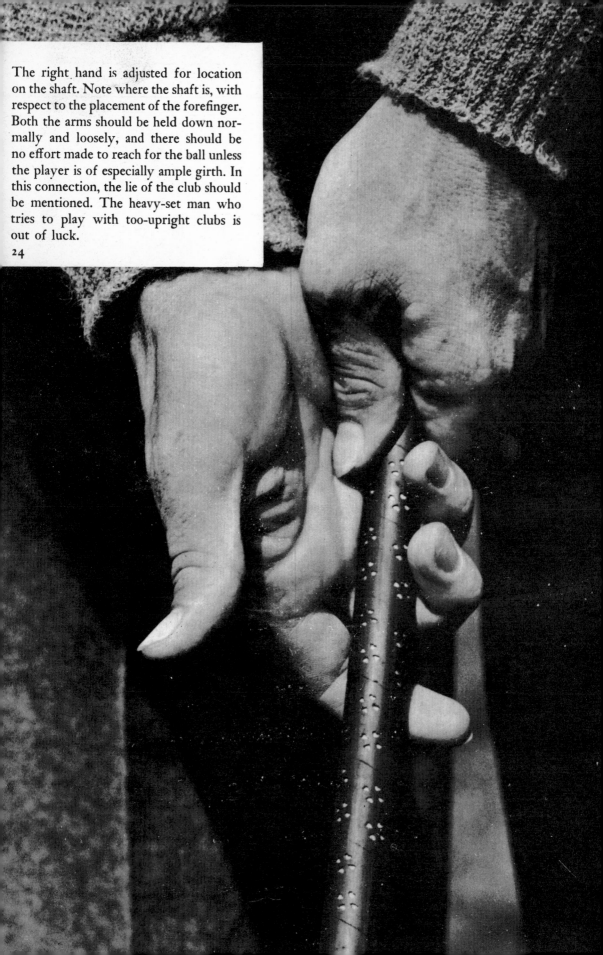

The right hand is adjusted for location on the shaft. Note where the shaft is, with respect to the placement of the forefinger. Both the arms should be held down normally and loosely, and there should be no effort made to reach for the ball unless the player is of especially ample girth. In this connection, the lie of the club should be mentioned. The heavy-set man who tries to play with too-upright clubs is out of luck.

24

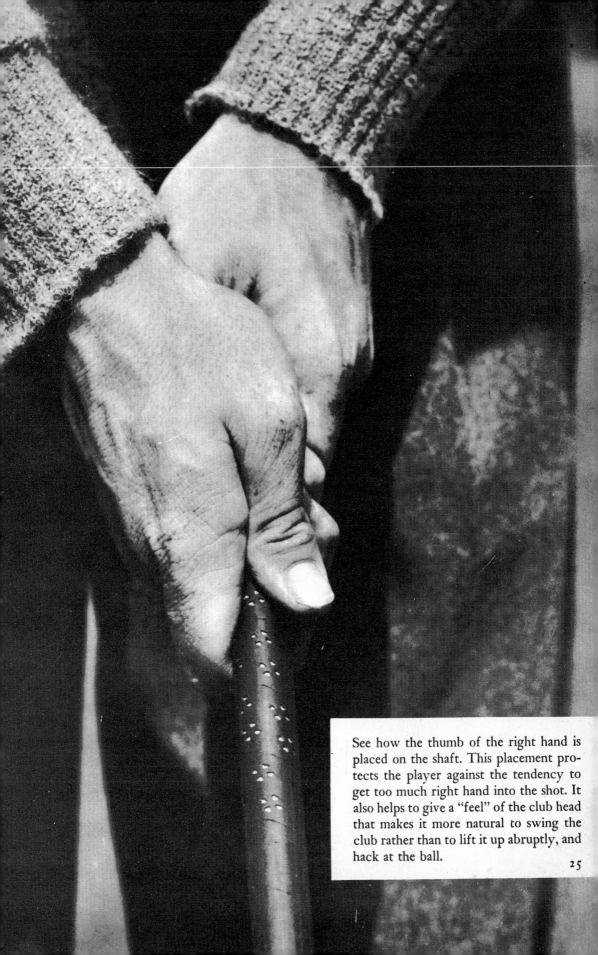

See how the thumb of the right hand is placed on the shaft. This placement protects the player against the tendency to get too much right hand into the shot. It also helps to give a "feel" of the club head that makes it more natural to swing the club rather than to lift it up abruptly, and hack at the ball.

25

Notice that the little finger of your right hand lies on top and across the first finger of your left hand. This grip I've been explaining may feel a little awkward for a while but practice with it, and you'll soon agree that it helps your shots.

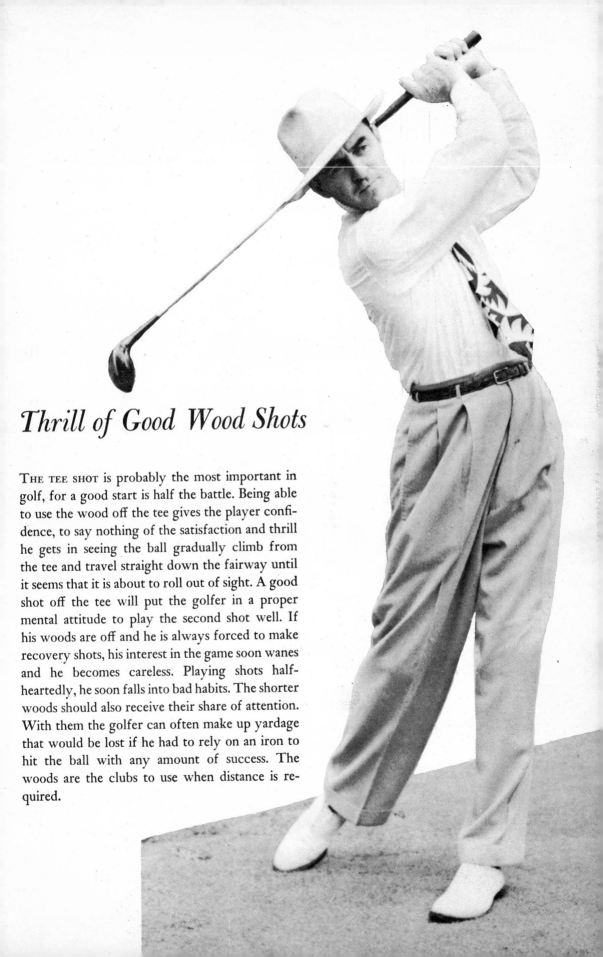

Thrill of Good Wood Shots

THE TEE SHOT is probably the most important in golf, for a good start is half the battle. Being able to use the wood off the tee gives the player confidence, to say nothing of the satisfaction and thrill he gets in seeing the ball gradually climb from the tee and travel straight down the fairway until it seems that it is about to roll out of sight. A good shot off the tee will put the golfer in a proper mental attitude to play the second shot well. If his woods are off and he is always forced to make recovery shots, his interest in the game soon wanes and he becomes careless. Playing shots half-heartedly, he soon falls into bad habits. The shorter woods should also receive their share of attention. With them the golfer can often make up yardage that would be lost if he had to rely on an iron to hit the ball with any amount of success. The woods are the clubs to use when distance is required.

Various Uses of Wood Clubs

WHEN PLAYING A WOOD SHOT, remember a straight ball pays off over the one that is slugged farther but winds up in the rough. Instructors will always warn the novice against trying to hit too far. To achieve distance, the player should try to swing more freely; then the movements will be more accurately made. The more accuracy, the farther the ball will travel. Any form of pressing will cut down distance.

There is no question that the shot off the tee is more easily made than one made when the ball is lying on the fairway. The ball is more easily struck, and no unusual demands are made on the player when it is set up well. When this situation presents itself on the fairway, the stroke used off the tee is the one to use — striking the ball well in the back so that it will run. But when the ball has found a difficult lie, there are variations that must be made, and the sweeping shot used off the tee will not always get the ball into the air. The brassie shot off the fairway must be played from where it lies. This is one disadvantage over the tee shot, where the player can select the position and placement of the ball.

There are times when the golfer will find that his ball is not setting up well, and that he cannot rely on the stroke he used off the tee. If the lie is close, he should study it to see if a wood shot is justified. The chances of failing are great, if the lie is too close to use a wood; the player then would be better off to use an iron. For a wood, there should be a clear path for the clubhead to swing into the ball. If the lie is cupped, the iron should be used, for with its more upright swing, the clubhead can be brought down sharper and the ball can be more solidly hit than if a wood were used with a blow that has a longer arc.

The golfer confronted with a close lie should hit down with the brassie. To get a brassie shot up, the same rules apply as in getting an iron shot into the air. It is the loft of the club and a downward blow, plus backspin, that will cause the ball to rise. The ball will not rise as quickly as when hit with an iron, so be sure there is enough room in front. If there is not, the player should use the spoon or No. 4 wood. Needing a longer stroke than the iron, the brassie rarely takes a divot, but just strips the sod in front of the ball.

28

If there is any doubt as to whether the brassie should be used on a particular shot, it is better to use the spoon. The spoon, being a shorter club, will bring the golfer closer to the ball and the swing will be more upright. Naturally the ball will have to be played slightly more toward the right foot so that it can be caught while the clubhead is still descending. A good position for the ball is at a point between the center of the stance and the left heel.

It is important when playing shots off the fairway to start the backswing smoothly, and not to hurry the downswing. Free the body of any tension that may have crept into it by the thought that you are going to miss the shot; have the same confidence as you would off the tee, where the ball is teed up. It is true the latter is easier, and that swinging is much smoother and a more simple matter, but if you will remember the important thing about golf — to get the ball up in in the air, hit down on it — you will soon gain the necessary confidence, and shots off the fairway will cease to worry you.

The Stance

BALANCE is the very beginning of any golf shot. Stand with your weight evenly divided and your legs not too far apart. Turn the toes of both feet outward because this helps you retain good balance throughout your swing. Have your arms hanging freely so the movement of your body doesn't interfere with your arms. The ball and the hands are practically in the same vertical plane.

I drive with a slightly open stance; with the left foot a bit farther away than the right one from the line of intended flight. Others prefer a square stance, with both feet equi-distant from the line, and there are many excellent players who use a closed stance with the right foot farther away from the line. This, so the champions of the closed stance maintain, makes it easier to hit from inside the line of flight in an arc out into the ball. Such an arc, of course, is proper, except in the cases of deliberate slices and "cut" shots.

Note that the knees are loose in the address.

A few waggles to get loosened up, and to get the flow of the swing started without a jerk, are really an important part of the swing. They help you to feel the beginning of a smooth swing. Then you easily work into the first stage of the swing, which is illustrated here.

A slight lift of the left heel starts the hips rotating away from the shot. The left arm is held straight, practically as an extension of the shaft. There is no effort at all made to lift the club from the ground. The club head is kept low.

The left knee begins to bend slightly toward the right and there is a noticeable straightening of the right leg, although there should be no feeling of the right knee locking.

In this initial stage of the swing the prevention of tightening up is highly important. You can make many perfect swings clipping dandelions and scraps of paper, but when a golf ball is before you you're apt to become tense to a degree that completely destroys your precision. Take it easily and lazily, because the golf ball isn't going to run away from you while you're swinging.

Get your "master eye" drawing a bead on the ball. This determines the proper position of your head. Being careful about sighting your shot helps you, subconsciously, to concentrate. Your head will stay still enough if you do the other things right.

The Drive

The ball in this series of pictures on the drive appears to be played almost even with the right heel, although the angle at which the picture was taken accounts for that. The ball actually is played slightly ahead of the center of the stance.

32

See how the left shoulder and hip begin to sli downward and around as on a banked turn of track. It greatly simplifies it for the average play if he will think almost altogether about left s performance in the earlier stages of instructic because it is the left that seems to be the maj factor in precision.

Note how balance has been maintained from t feet upward. The right foot is firmly planted a the inside of the left instep is pushing the hi around in their pivot. Note, also, how the left kn stays in the same horizontal plane instead of di ping as it does so frequently in the cases of hig handicap players.

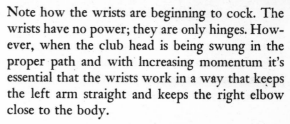

ow the hands and arms begin to do some de-
erate work in completing the backswing. Keep
e left arm as straight as it is naturally, but don't
ghten up by trying to get a feeling of tensity
that arm or you'll be inclined to take it out of
e shot and do the rest of the work with your
dy, and get a dead swing.

e body continues to swing around, as may be
served by study of the position of the right leg
this picture and the one preceeding. The left
m is bent slightly but retains a feeling of down-
rd tension. Note the position of the hands,
tually the same as in the address. No roll of the
rearms has occurred.

Note how the wrists are beginning to cock. The
wrists have no power; they are only hinges. However, when the club head is being swung in the
proper path and with increasing momentum it's
essential that the wrists work in a way that keeps
the left arm straight and keeps the right elbow
close to the body.

As the top of the swing is neared the player's hips
have completed almost a 90 degree turn from the
address position. This isn't possible for the older
and less supple player, but the cocking of the
wrists as shown, is not difficult, and it is important for securing power and firmness in the shot.

33

Note that the shaft of the club has begun to drop below horizontal. That also is something that isn't advisable for the less flexible player, although the fullest extent of a wrist-cocking that can be attained without losing control of the club, is highly desirable.

Here the major feature is from the hips up, with the shoulders coming around. There is a feeling of a definite pull on the left shoulder and arm. The knees are bent to allow freedom that promotes speed on the downswing. The angle of the wrists with the forearms is the same as it was at the top of the backswing.

You will note from the position of the knees th the downward motion of the body already h started, although from the position of the han and club shaft it is plain that the club has ju reached the farthest point of its backswing. common error is to start back with the arms befo the pivot has been completed.

Now the hips are almost parallel with the li of intended flight. The wrists have begun straighten out into line with the arms. Note ho the right elbow is down, and stays comfortab close to the body.

34

Now note how the knees are beginning to bend in a sort of a "sitting down to the ball" position, while there has been only a very slight change in the position of the club. The fraction of a second pause at the top of the backswing is caused unconsciously and is a sign that the wrists are not beginning to break too soon.

See how the left heel is settling down to a firm anchorage. From watching all the good ones hit, I've got the idea that this is one of the very important details of the long shotmaking. Simply getting that left foot well planted seems to be the action that controls the rest of the leg and body performance.

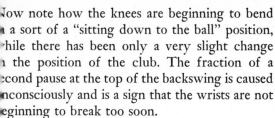

The left leg begins to straighten so it will be in the same position as at address. The wrists are snapping into a straight line with the arms so the club head will be brought through its wide arc, into the ball at the right time. This hand action has brought the shoulders around properly.

See how the right leg seems to be shoving power into the shot. The camera angle of this shot is misleading. Actually the ball, the hands, and the left shoulder are almost in a straight line, as they were at address. Note how the right shoulder has dropped and the left one raised, as the swing approaches a vertical plane.

35

Note how the club head is whipped through after the ball. There has been no conscious effort to roll the right wrist over; in fact, the right palm is kept square to the ball almost like a handball shot, as long as it can naturally and comfortably stay square.

The right shoulder has come down and under a way similar to its action in throwing a baseba underhanded. The right wrist starts to turn ov because the plane of the club head travel is chan ing from vertical to an inclined plane.

It's simply a matter of smoothly "coasting" now. The hips start to turn square to the hole.

36

Observe how the hands finish high. In the case a smaller and heavier player, the finish would at a lower point.

e how the hips continue to be almost in the me position they occupied when the club head et the ball. This means that the body has stayed hind the shot, and is an indication that the club ad has been lashed through the ball with the nds and arms.

The follow-through has reached its effective maximum in indicating that all possible power and control has been given to the shot. See how firm the left and right feet are staying to the ground, thus giving evidence that balance has been retained.

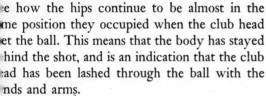

e how gradually the head has been brought up. here has been no jerking upward of the head by correct action of hands and arms.

The club finished far around because there has been no tendency to "brake" the club after the ball has been hit. Momentum carries the club.

37

The arms are hanging easily and almost straigh
down. The club is soled flat on the ground. Ther
is no aspect of tensity about any phase of th
starting position.

The Drive SIDE VIEW

Up to this point there has been no conscious move
ment of the hands. They have followed the pivo
automatically. Note, especially the way the hip
are swinging around in response to left leg impulse

Note that the feet are in a line parallel with the line of intended flight. However, it suits some players to have either the right or left foot slightly farther away from the line, for drives and other shots.

Watch how the position of the hands is kept low. The club head is started back by the left leg beginning the pivot. The left shoulder and arm follow the action from the foot up.

Here's where the cocking of the wrists begins. See how the left foot shows that the swing is depending a lot on pressure from the ball of the left foot.

By comparing the position of the club head here, with that in the preceding picture, you get the idea of how far a slight cocking of the wrists moves the club head.

39

The right elbow is held close, but not tightly, to the body; with the elbow pointing down. Watch how the back of the left hand keeps approximately parallel with the face of the club.

See how the left shoulder and the left forearm position show the way to get a long sweep that is a necessary item in getting a powerful shot. Watch, too, how the right leg is braced as the axis of the swing.

Observe that a sort of a "sitting down" action has taken place. This prepares one for getting the body "punch" timed along with the legs, arms, and wrists, and protects against tensity.

40

Now the left leg has begun to straigten out so the hit can be made on a firm axis. The left shoulder is still under the chin but is drawing the club head down. Wrists continue to be cocked.

e wrists have done almost all of the moving of club head that's been accomplished since the evious picture. They're getting into position uncocking to whip the club head at the ball.

Note that the club head, wrists, and arms are about in the same position as in the previous picture, but that body action has started, as is evident from comparing knee positions. The downswing starts with the left leg.

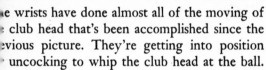

this point both feet are flat on the ground to vide a good balance for the club head speed increase without throwing the club head out focus on its target. Here is where you want to in uncocking your wrists.

Note how far the shoulders have moved since the preceding position, but with the wrists in the same relative position. Compare this picture with the one just ahead of it. The wrists uncocking have brought the club head through space too fast for the camera to catch the club head. Note how the left leg is braced. **41**

There has been a straightening of the right leg and a full lash in uncocking the wrists as the ball is hit. See how close to a straight line the left shoulder, hands, and club head are.

The ball is on its way and the club head poir after it. You can see in this picture that plenty power has been poured into the shot by the rig arm, but that it's kept in line by the straight le

See how the head has been brought up naturally. What makes the head jerk up prematurely generally is faulty arm action rather than a hasty curiosity to see where the shot has gone.

42

The grip remains firm all through the swing, cluding the follow-through.

oserve that the hips have been almost in the ne position for the last four views. That means : hitting has been done from a hub that has yed fixed in about the position of the base of : spine.

The right arm is staying just as straight as the left one did on the backswing. The wrists are turning over because they have to; the momentum of the club head swinging around and up makes them.

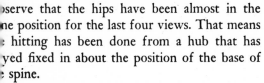

e second half of the follow-through comes au- natically. If it's easy and approximately in the th of these pictures, it's a tip-off that the back-

swing and hit were correct. The follow-through is, in many respects, a reversed pattern of the backswing.

43

Action of the Feet

A PROFESSIONAL can look at a player's feet in action, and can nearly always tell what is wrong with the stroke. Foot action is one of the main differences between a good golfer and a duffer.

As the hands reach about halfway in the backswing, correct foot action has the weight of the body shifted against the right foot. The left heel has left the ground, with the ball of the left foot maintaining the balance.

At this same position the duffer makes the mistake of shifting all the weight onto the right foot by a lateral hip movement. When the top of the swing is reached, the left heel is drawn so high that the foot is almost at right angles to the ground. The toe then supports only the weight of the foot, rather than aiding the ball of the foot to grasp the ground and maintain balance. Starting the downswing with the feet in this position, the duffer can only make the fatal mistake, "failing to return the left heel to the ground." The left foot then is not in position to receive the weight about to be thrust upon it. When the weight is kept on the right foot the hips cannot turn out of the way to allow the hands to swing past. With the hips blocking the hands, power is lost.

When foot action has been faulty the duffer is hitting flatfooted. The expert on the other hand finds that at impact the right heel has left the ground and the foot is pushing against a resisting force. Although terrific force thrown against the left leg in the downswing may slightly roll the left foot over, it is firmly set, receiving the weight which has been shifted against it.

perfect shot and follow-through will leave one a well balanced position.

ot and leg position at the top of the backswing. ote location of ball for wood shot. See how the essure is being applied from the ball of the left ot. Left knee is swung to the right; not dipped.

Downswing has started. Weight is being transferred from the right foot to the left. Observe how the knees still are bent slightly so straightening them will add impetus to club head and power to the shot.

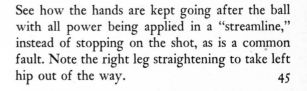

t for the shot. The left leg is straight and the nds are whipping the club head through. Note w the hips are sliding through, rather than turn-, as compared with previous position.

See how the hands are kept going after the ball with all power being applied in a "streamline," instead of stopping on the shot, as is a common fault. Note the right leg straightening to take left hip out of the way. 45

The Long Irons

ONE MIGHT CALL IRON PLAY the fine part of the game. A golfer does not slug with irons as he does with woods, nor does he try to achieve great distances. Iron clubs are designed for accuracy, and that should be the aim when playing them. The shafts are shorter than those fitted to the woods — necessitating a stance closer to the ball to provide for a rounder and more upright swing.

The No. 1, No. 2, and No. 3 irons are called the long irons. It is true that they are used to attain a certain distance, but the distance is considerably less than that which can be acquired with the woods. They are the clubs to use when the lie on the fairway does not permit the use of the wood club, and yet a maximum distance is desired.

Some golfers prefer to use a No. 4 wood in preference to the long irons. It is a good club to use on a calm day, for the degree of pitch of the club will send the ball high in the air, and a green can be held. But if the elements are disturbing, it is far safer to use the long iron. The ball is hit lower and the wind effect on the flight of the ball will be lessened.

Since the stroke is one in which the ball is struck a downward blow, there is a minimum chance that the ball will be sliced or hooked. If correctly hit, the backspin applied to the ball will hold it on the correct line.

When to Use the Long Irons

IRON PLAY is the core of the golf game. It is the middle stroke on which a continuation of the success off the tee depends, or on which a handicap from that spot is overcome. This shot requires more skill than the stroke played off the tee. It is a shot that requires considerable thinking. It demands mental calculation in advance, so that the player will have a definite object in mind.

The long iron is used when the shot calls for distance, plus accuracy, and it stresses the latter. It is the club that gets you there, if the right club is used for the right distance.

A straight-faced club is used when the lie is so close on the fairway that the use of a wood is prohibited. Being a shorter stick, greater accuracy is attained with it.

Irons are played for position, and if the shot is more easily played with a longer iron, that is the club to use. Avoid under-clubbing. A mashie-niblick, with a full swing, should not be used when the shot calls for a mashie with a three-quarter swing; neither should a No. 5 iron be used when the mid-iron is called for.

A half swing with a club suited for the distance is far more likely to be accurate than will be overswinging with a club not designed for the length. The shorter the swing, the more accurate will be the shot. There is little glory in hitting a 180 yard mashie shot. The idea is to see how close to the pin you can put the ball.

The long iron is a good club to use when the shot has to be played into the wind. The straight face will keep the ball low where the elements will not have the effect they have on a shot hit higher into the air. Clubs are designed with a variation of ten yards distance, so it is a good idea, when playing against the wind, to use a club one mark stronger than that used on a calm day.

In the long iron play, a loose grip must be avoided. You might get away with a looser grip off the tee, but here a firm grip is very necessary. Since the shock is greater in hitting the iron, a loose grip often can cause the club to turn in the player's hands.

The stance for iron play has an important part in achieving the desired results. An open stance is used because the goal is not distance. This stance shortens the backstroke and the pivot and the backswing become more compact, giving the player greater accuracy.

The long iron shot differs from the wood in that the stance is closer to the ball — a position necessitated by the shorter shaft. This brings the body closer to the ball so that the swing is more upright. Greater accuracy is then obtained. The ball should be played from a position in which it can be hit a downward blow. The upright swing makes it easier to do this than if the arc of the swing is a flat one.

Fundamentals of the swing are the same. The club should be taken back slowly and close to the ground, and the downstroke should be started in the same manner as with the wood.

Although the turn of the hips is restricted, do not consciously shorten the backswing; there should be a full and free shoulder turn. At the top of the swing, the position of the club is similar to that for the wood, but the hands should never go back beyond the shoulders. As already stated, this shot is not one for maximum length. That is achieved with the woods.

The long iron is one of the most important shots in the game, for if it is played well and onto the green, an extra chip shot is not necessary.

The stance is not quite as wide as for the wood club shots. The ball is about 3 inches back of a line to the left heel. Your grip is slightly stronger than with a wood shot, but not tense.

Keep the club head low when you're swinging back, and you'll be sure to swing, instead of trying to pick up the club and chop at the ball. See how the head is cocked and left eye is drawing bead on the ball.

The Long Irons

Note how the left shoulder has come around under the chin. The head has been held still as you can see from inspecting that showing of shirt above the neck of my sweater. No reason for the head to move; the legs, body, and wrists are doing the work.

Here you see where the correct grip shows its importance. There is no rolling of the wrists so the club head is held in position.

50

ote the straight line from the left shoulder to e club head. Try to remember that and you'll ercome the temptation to lift the club with ur hands. The picture angle shows the ball far- er back than it really is.

The wrist cocking begins at this point (just as in the wood club swing). Study the way the legs work so the right hip swings easily out of the way, and permits a free, smooth swing.

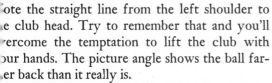

ee how the left arm is held out straight, so the llest arc of the backswing can be secured. The hole idea of the backswing is to windup for a lease of power without any jerkiness, going or ming.

Observe how the wrists have cocked almost 45 degrees from the preceding picture, while there has been relatively little change in the rest of the elements making up the backswing.

51

You can see from this picture that the action of the right hip shows a rotation instead of a swaying back along a fairly straight line away from the ball. This proper action makes it easier to hit harder.

You will see that the shaft of the iron club doesn't go much lower than horizontal and the pivot for the irons is less than for the woods.

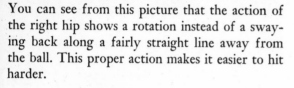

See how the left arm is stretched to the full length of its leverage in providing power for the shot, and to avoid any change in the path of the club head that might result from an uncertain angle in the elbow.

See how the legs are beginning to straighten up from a "sitting down" position so the hit may be made with the left leg firm and straight. Notice, also that there has been no uncocking of the wrists. The ball is under the head. There is no swaying of the body.

52

Note that both wrists are under the shaft at the top of the swing. All these pictures are separated by the same time interval, so you will observe that there is a pause of the club head at the top of the swing so the downswing will be smooth.

Watch the knee action in this series of pictures. You will see that the body has begun its action for the downswing while the hands continue to be held at the top. Many players lose power and control by starting the hands first on the downswing.

At this point the swing path becomes more vertical. The body has about completed its work of swinging around on the hips and begins to set itself, so the hand action can proceed smoothly and whip down at the ball.

When the shaft gets at this point — level with the ground — then the wrists begin to shoot the works. From this stage of the swing down to the point of impact comes a good part of the power of the shot which results from speed of club head travel.

53

The club head is traveling too fast for the speed camera to catch because the wrists have lashed the club head at the farthest point of the swing's arc. Note how the right arm has straightened out to keep the club head in the right path.

See how the left hip is rising, rather than rotating. That means the left leg has been kept straight as a fixed point for the critical center of this part of the swing. The wrists haven't rolled. The back of the left hand is square to the line of flight.

Observe how balance has been maintained clear through to the finish of the shot. If you fall forward or away in your follow-through you can be sure you haven't made the best possible shot, regardless of where the ball goes.

Now your right arm swings all the way around fully outstretched.

54

ote how the arms seem to be almost flying out
their sockets. They can talk all they want about
e follow-through not being an important part
the stroke, but when your follow-through
turally takes your club head after the ball you
n be sure that you've got power and direction.

Now the wrists begin to turn over because the
arms have reached the limit of possible stretch
after the shot. In being carried around by momentum, they make every element of the swing co-
ordinate properly. Note how the club head is
finishing high.

e sure your follow-through is an integral part
your swing and not merely added to it.

The Mashie

The most versatile club in the average player's bag is the mashie, when it's allowed to do its work without being handicapped by a tendency to scoop the ball. Hit down at it.

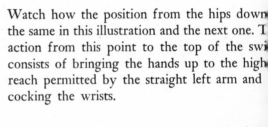

The ball is played a few inches back of a line even with the left heel; not as far back as shown in these pictures. These pictures were taken from about even with my right shoulder to get in more details of knee, shoulder, and hand action.

See how the hands are kept low. Don't try to ￼ the club. The angles of club lofts are figured ￼ get the ball up off the ground, if you will let the ￼ function naturally. Watch the hip position w ￼ respect to the light triangle in the background ￼

The Mashie

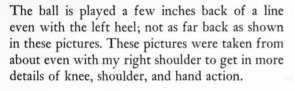

Note that there has been no rolling over of the right arm. The line of the shoulders is almost at right angles to the line of intended flight. See that reach with the left arm; it's straight but it isn't tense.

Watch how the position from the hips down ￼ the same in this illustration and the next one. T ￼ action from this point to the top of the swi ￼ consists of bringing the hands up to the high ￼ reach permitted by the straight left arm and ￼ cocking the wrists.

58

you will keep your knees on a fairly level plane, tead of dipping the left knee, you'll be far more rtain of a correct pivot. The impetus for the ot feels like it comes from inside the left foot, th the left heel being lifted only enough to ke action comfortable.

The right leg has straightened and the right hip is being swung out of the way, so the backswing can proceed smoothly with the left arm straight and the right elbow kept fairly close to the body. The wrists are cocking.

is is the top of the mashie swing. Note that e club's shaft is level with the ground and that e head still is over the ball, just as it was in the dressing. You must feel firmly balanced but not cked, at this point. The grip must be firm but xible here.

See how the shoulders have turned even though the club hasn't changed position from the previous illustration. The left knee has started toward its eventual straight position.

The left foot has come down flat on the ground. There is a feeling of squatting that comes from a change from a fairly flat to an upright arc of the swing. That "sitting down" to the ball keeps the body from getting so stiff it interferes with a free swing.

See how the left side is beginning to feel firm a get anchored to allow a tremendous hit with hands without jerking the player off balance. T body change must be made without letting right elbow get far away from the body.

Compare this picture with an illustration of a wood coming into contact with the ball. Then you will see how the mashie shot is more upright, with a snap down into the ball and dependence on the loft of the club to make the ball rise in its correct trajectory.

60

See the divot flying out behind the club he This means that the ball was hit a descending bl and that the club was carried on through with grip being firm enough to make a clean slash the sod without the wrists being rolled over the arms slowed up with a jerk.

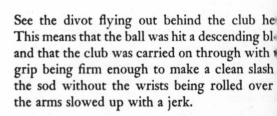

ote that the wrists are in the same position as ey were at the top of the swing. The right knee starting to straighten so the legs, at the moment impact, will be a firm foundation for the body, ns, and hands performance.

Right here you will see how the wrists are acting at the beginning of a whipping motion. From this point on through the ball, there should be feeling that the wrists are uncocking with a snap at the ends of straight arms.

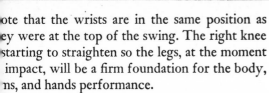

ain the club head reaches after the ball and e right arm is as straight in the follow-through the left one was in the backswing. When you t those arms working correctly, with the elbows ld almost the same distance apart throughout e swing, you cure a lot of troubles.

See how the left side moves out of the way quickly. The feet are closer together in a mashie shot than with longer irons or woods, hence it should be easier for you to keep to the path of the swing instead of trying to do tricks with your knees. **61**

Finishing this way brings considerable relaxation of the right side.

Just let the hands complete the fling of the cl and if you've been properly balanced and y grip is right you'll finish the shot smoothly firmly.

n't "loop" the club head at the finish of the ing.

Let your straight right arm keep the club swinging in a wide arc away from your body.

Note how closely to the body the hands are held. The sole of the club is flat on the ground. Your eyes, hands, and toes are in the same line: Knees are slightly bent.

The right side is being slid back and around, of the way. The club head is being swung by t arms, and not lifted by the wrists. The should and arms are being moved around by foot, l and knee action.

Mashie Shot SIDE VIEW

See at the top of the backswing how the hands are under the club, and because the grip is right there hasn't been any loosening of control of the club. You're ready to pull down with your left arm.

A decided pull with the left arm has brought t right elbow in closer to the body. Note how swi ly the hips are getting into a line with the hc compared with slow change in shaft position.

64

atch the left knee with respect to the patch of
ht ahead of it. The knee doesn't dip. The right
is straightening and the hips are swinging
und. Wrist cocking begins slowly here.

Now the wrists are beginning to cock rapidly.
At this point you should be looking over your left
shoulder at the ball so that you may feel your left
shoulder touch your chin.

w the left foot has come down flat on the
und and is set for allowing the left arm and
ulder to work from a steady axis in getting
club head on the right track back to the ball.

From this point on to the farthest out point of
the follow-through, watch how the right arm
straightens out. See how the left leg works now,
just about as the right one did in the backswing.

65

Here the wrists start to uncock with all the limberness and speed that can be attained with the proper grip. Watch the hips lift a little and note how the club comes from inside the line of flight to the ball.

Observe that the hands are low and how the club head is going down below the ball. Note how close the right elbow is to the body. The left is braced so the power for hitting has a so anchorage.

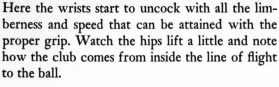

The right shoulder action in this follow-through shows you what happens when you correctly hit down at, and through, a mashie shot instead of trying to scoop it up.

66

The club head has pulled the hands and arms w around in a wide arc.

he hands go through after the ball. You can
e that by watching how the right arm is straight
d brings the right shoulder down rather than
ound on a horizontal plane.

Your weight is well on your left foot here, and
you hit up against your left hip.

is shot ends with weight on left leg and right
e of body and right leg released.

The Short Irons

When to Use Pitching Clubs

THE PITCH SHOT is probably the most spectacular in golf. I know of no other shot that gives me more thrill than to spank a high rising shot and see its backspin halt the ball near the hole. Pitching is invaluable to good scoring, for it is the pitch laid in the vicinity of the flag that affords the player the opportunity to birdie the hole.

The pitching clubs are those graduated from the mashie to the niblick. The shafts are of different lengths. The heads have a varying degree of loft (much more than the longer irons), enabling the player to impart more backspin to the ball. The player will find them easier to play, for, as already stated, in long iron play, as the golfer stands closer to the ball, the stroke becomes rounder and is more accurately made.

The stance for these pitching clubs gets narrower and more open as the shorter sticks are used. It is closer to the ball until the use of the putter brings the player's head directly over the ball. If the player will remember this, he will have little trouble with pitching clubs.

Since little pivot is used, control of the club must be in the hands and arms. Never reach for the ball when playing this shot.

It is not necessary to take a long swing. A little practice with these clubs, starting fifty yards from the green and working back, will soon give the player the range for each club, and an idea as to the length of backswing necessary for the needed distance.

ONE MIGHT CALL these clubs the trouble clubs. They are used in the rough when a bad lie presents itself and it is necessary to get the ball out of sand. When the ball lies close to the green, but has found a shaggy lie, they fill the bill. A chip cannot be made out of long grass.

If the ball requires extraction from heavy rough, you can bank on a well-lofted club to do the job. The player will be wise, if he selects a more lofted club when the lie is heavy, and attempts to cut under the ball. There will be little chance for applying backspin, so don't attempt to hold the green with this shot. Allow for a good margin of run.

70

WHEN TO USE PITCHING CLUBS

When a bunker lies in the way, the pitch is the shot to use. Golfers often use the mashie or mashie-niblick on this shot, but when a shorter distance makes a crisp firm shot with these clubs impossible, the niblick is used. There is a distinct advantage in playing a longer approach, for the ball can be firmly hit and a full swing taken. However, it is sometimes necessary to play half shots and three-quarter shots. Under 120 yards, at which point the full niblick is used, the golfer must depend on his ability in varying the stroke so that it will give the desired effect. The ball should be hit firmly, yet must not over-run the green. To accomplish this, move the hands down the leather as the shot becomes shorter.

Greens are built for pitching. They are watered and are softer than the surrounding area. But if they are hard and fast, sometimes it is impossible to hold them, no matter how much backspin is applied. It is then better to use a pitch-and-run shot, aiming at a spot in front of the green and letting the ball run up to the hole. The shot is played with a club with less loft than would normally be called for.

There will be times when the golfer will have to pitch over a trap, and the distance will be so short that the full-hit backspin shot cannot be used; neither can he run the ball through the trap. A niblick should be used and a slice spin be added to make the ball stop with the least run. Lay the face of the club back a little on this shot. A great fault here is indecision — don't baby the shot or "wish" the ball up to the hole.

Set your weight evenly on both feet. The short iron shots, being strokes with comparatively little body turn, need steady arm action.

No wrists in the shot yet. The straight left ar swings the club back easily, smoothly. Both fe are on the ground throughout the backswing.

The Short Irons

You get all the stretch you can with the left arm in the short iron shots, just the same as you do with the longer iron and wood shots.

See how there's very little body action in th three pictures showing the uppermost part of th swing. It's wrist action here.

ee how the right elbow stays in close. About
hen the shaft points at your right pocket, begin
cock your wrists.

Note there's been very little action of the left
knee. The short iron swings are very upright, but
must be made inside the line of flight.

ee how the wrists hinge without any rolling
:tion of the arm to take the club face out of its
roper facing.

The left shoulder starts to move away from the
chin. Note that the left foot is flat and firm on the
ground.

73

By keeping the body action at a minimum the short iron swing is kept upright, and the loft of the clubs is correctly employed.

Here the left leg begins to brace, smoothly, wh the left shoulder is bringing the club down to ball. Wrists are not uncocked.

Note that the left shoulder has not been lifted from the time in the preceding picture when the wrists began to uncock. Stay down to the ball.

74

See that the same firm left side has been maintai to hit against. The turf has been hit after the b The down blow raises the ball.

ote there's no evidence of tensity, even though e short iron shots often are recovery shots. The ree-quarter swing must not be rushed.

Now the wrists begin to uncock. It's from this point down to the ball that the snap comes for power.

he right side relaxes in order that the follow-rough will be smooth and full, and that the ctor of precision be kept.

Now the arms and wrists are rolling because the body is turning square to the hole. Note how full arm leverage is used to the end.

75

If you have hit down on the ball properly, the ball will have plenty of backspin.

Keep hitting the short iron shot. If you have quit on the shot you'll have a full follow-through.

ractice this shot a lot. Expertness with your short
ons will save you many strokes.

As in other shots, finish this swing with a firm
grip on the club.

Due to the lie of the club and length of shaft you have to bend over more than with longer club shots. Get your head almost over the ball.

Observe how far inside the line of flight the club head comes without any action of the wrists in lifting the club. The feet are firm.

Short Iron Shot SIDE VIEW

The action is similar to that of coiling a spring; you wind up from the hips until your shoulders and wrists get the club back.

78

Now the wrists are cocked so the club is about at a 45 degree angle with the ground. Three quarters of a swing is all you need in this.

Watch the shoulders and the wrists start to do the work at this point. There's not much knee-action in the short iron swing.

The straight left arm is the main feature of control of the shot from this point back and down, but the right elbow shouldn't stray.

The "sitting down" motion is less pronounced in the short iron shots, but it still is an element in getting punch into the blow.

Throughout this series of short iron pictures you're bound to note that the shot is upright; a hit rather than a swing.

79

Observe how the right arm is straightening even though it continues to be held close to the body. The shoulders are working strongly.

Now the wrists have begun to straighten out both arms and wrists will be parallel to the cl grip when the ball is hit.

Watch the right arm show its place in putting power into the shot. The left is virtually an extension of the club shaft.

80

A complete follow-through is a sign that the sho has been hit crisply. You have to hit short iror firmly; the loft kills distance.

et the left side out of the way so the ball can be t sharply without any interference from the dy.

See how the ball has jumped up quickly, although club head has just reached the grass level after hitting down and is taking a divot.

There's no speed in lifting the head in the follow-through because it comes up naturally, and at the right time in response to the proper arm and shoulder action.

81

The Explosion Shot

THE FOREMOST THOUGHT which should be in the player's mind when his ball is lying in a bunker is: Be sure to get it out!

There is more than one way of playing recovery shots, but if the trap is deep, if the ball is buried or has found a heel print, methods other than the explosion shot should be disregarded. It is true that the cut shot can be used under similar circumstances, but for safety, the explosion is the shot for the average player.

This shot is mainly used when the ball is to be placed from the trap onto the green, or from a trap close to the green. It is not used when the player requires distance.

First of all, anchor your feet firmly in the sand. Stand well over the ball.

Grip the club low and not at the top of the leather. Swing the club back with a straight left arm and firm wrists.

The Explosion Shot

From this point on to the top of the swing the action is mostly with the wrists, as you'll note from the shoulder positions.

84

By keeping the left arm extended you protect yourself against an inclination to try to scoop the ball up, or to hurry and jerk the shot.

ote that the ball is played off the left foot and
at the stance is open, with the left foot drawn
way from the intended line of flight.

The head must not move, and there's comparatively little leg action, because this is an exceed-
ingly upright swing.

atch the wrists cock, and see in this picture how
e right hand indicates that the face of the club
as been "opened" somewhat.

There's the usual very slight pause of all good
swings that you'll note at the top of this sand
niblick swing.   85

Observe how the club is hammered down with the shoulders and wrists until the club head digs into the sand well behind the ball. The distance the sand is hit behind the ball determines the length of the shot; however you must judge the firmness and texture of the sand, which you can do when you wiggle your feet around getting a

firm stance. The same straight left on the backswing, with the right elbow in, and the transfer to the straight right in the follow-through, takes place in this shot, as it does in other iron and wood shots.

In the explosion shots the follow-through is highly important. If you get into your mind that you are going through after the shot, you will really hit into it instead of letting the first contact with the sand stop your blow and diminish the effect on the ball.

The Explosion Shot SIDE VIEW

Note how the face of the club is laid back so it will have its greatest power from below when coming into the sand back and under the ball.

The explosion shot is one in which the club head is swung outside the line of intended flight and away from the body. This puts "cut" on the ball and stops it quickly after it lights.

90

In the explosion shots, come back with a bit more than a three-quarter swing, but don't be afraid to hit the ball. There is not much leg action. The feet, of course, stay firm in the sand. The straight left arm is highly important because it gives you the arc on the ball that otherwise would be hard to get when your club head is not permitted to

touch the ground, as the rules of golf apply to hazards. The left arm and the wrists play the greater part of this shot. The right arm, when its elbow is held close to the body, straightens out automatically when the proper spot in the downswing is reached.

The weight shifts from the right leg to the left one as the club comes down to the ball. Note how the swift action of the wrists near the bottom of the swing bring the face of the club in and across the ball, which normally would impart a slice to the ball.

However, the effect is smothered by the sand that's between the club face and the ball, and the actual result is to pop the ball up into the air and make it fall dead.
Seldom does the average player make consistently satisfactory recovery shots because

he's afraid to hit at the ball hard enough automatically to get a full, firm follow-through. This is no shot to chop and quit on; your excess of power — if you have any — will be safely absorbed by the sand.

The Putt

PUTTING is one department of the game the player should and can more easily round into shape. He can get it down to par figures more quickly than any other division of the game. Par allows thirty-six strokes on the putting surface per round, two on each hole.

It is on the greens that the final result of the hole is determined. It is the pay-off spot. Here a player can pick up a stroke that has been lost in playing from tee to green. But a stroke lost on the green is lost forever. There is nothing to make up after the first putt has been missed.

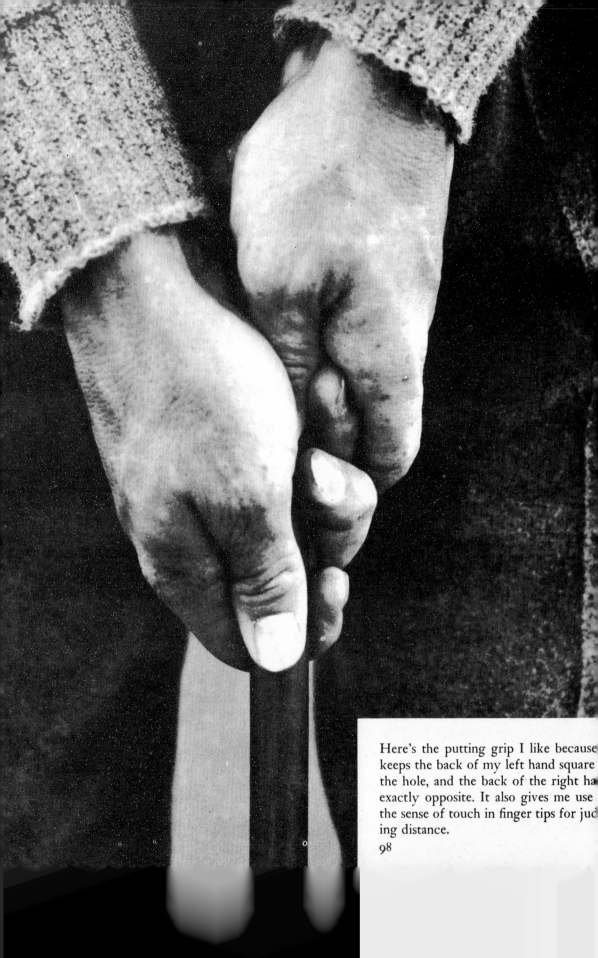

Here's the putting grip I like because keeps the back of my left hand square the hole, and the back of the right ha exactly opposite. It also gives me use the sense of touch in finger tips for jud ing distance.

Concentrate, Have Confidence, and Relax

AFTER THE PLAYER has learned the fundamental of the putting stroke, there are three important factors he should master — concentration, confidence, and relaxation.

Concentration is the most important, for the other two factors depend to a great extent on it. But just what concentration is, and how to achieve and put this faculty into use, is hard for the golfer to assimilate. Concentration is the faculty of being able to eliminate everything from the mind except the performance of the fundamental parts of the stroke — one at a time. This includes selecting the proper line to the hole, the proper stance and grip, and estimating correctly the length of the backswing. Having done these, the player now has confidence. This confidence is a self-assurance that the fundamentals have been correctly executed, so that the golfer needs only to think of the final act of swinging the putter — excluding all other thoughts from his mind.

With confidence, the player relaxes — and relaxation is conducive to good golf. It is hard to relax if one lacks confidence. When the player is not sure that he has correctly judged the line to the hole, or is worrying about his grip, he cannot stroke the ball smoothly. He is certain to attempt a last-second alteration of the stroke, upsetting the smooth, rhythmic swing.

Since the putting stroke depends so much on these three important factors, the golfer should experiment with his stance and stroke until he has found the one that is most comfortable; that is, the one, the fundamentals of which he will find easier to concentrate on, which gives him the confidence that results in relaxation.

The Putt

In putting get the line you want by coming up to the ball from the back, and studying the route. Then be sure that your putter blade is flat on the ground and squarely across the line so you can hit the ball firmly in the middle of the blade. That's the purpose for which your putter was designed. Get your left eye (if that's your master eye)

right over the ball. Have both toes even on a line parallel with that which you want the ball to travel when it leaves the club.

Hold your hands in close.

Putt the ball almost off the left toe, and keep the putter blade low to the ground. Have the blade stay square across the line as long as you can, comfortably, on the back-swing.

On a fast downhill putt, hold the club a bit looser than when you have to make an uphill putt.

The Putt FRONT VIEW

Observe how the left eye, the hands, and the ball are practically in a straight line. The knees are relaxed, but the body is held motionless and without tensity. The wrists do the work as you may observe from the spot of light near the left elbow. See how

easily, but firmly, the left arm is resting on the left leg.

When the putt is hit the left forearm slides gently and in a straight path, and the right hand follows with both hands in such position that, if they were opened, they would be squarely together. The head is held steady until well after the ball is hit. At no time is there body action in the putt.

Professional Tips
on How to Improve Your Score

Addressing the Ball

It is hard to keep one's balance when reaching for the ball . . . stand almost erect, letting the arms drop naturally from the shoulders.

SINCE THE POSITION at impact is similar to that taken at the start of the backswing it is important that the body and its parts are in the correct position before any action takes place. The player must be properly set, to get a good start toward a successful shot.

The distance one stands from the ball should be given consideration. A stance too far away flattens the swinging arc, requiring extreme finesse to have the club-head properly meet the ball square to the line. The position of the feet from the ball should vary according to the height and build of the individual. This is where the taller players have a slight advantage over the shorter ones; they can stand closer to the ball. This enables them to swing the club in a rounder, or more close to the vertical, arc, and greater accuracy is attained.

The feet should be comfortable. A good stance has the feet apart about the width of the shoulders. The weight should be evenly divided.

Stand fairly erect. Reaching must be avoided if balance throughout the swing is to be maintained. The arms and club should not form a straight line, but an angle. A good position at address has the arms falling naturally from the shoulders with the hands neither too close nor stretched out too far.

Since the stroke for the irons necessitates a downward blow, the swing is more upright, and the clubhead is brought down more abruptly on the ball. Move the feet closer together as the shorter clubs are used.

The Pivot

Shift the weight to the right foot in the backswing and turn the right hip to allow the hands to swing past.

THE PIVOT is probably the least understood of all golf actions. It is not just the twisting of the waist; neither is it the action of dropping the left shoulder toward the ball, as the duffer does.

Pivoting is the swinging of the club to the top of the backswing in a wide arc, with the left foot, knee, hip, and shoulder turning toward the right.

It is through this turning of the hips and shoulders that some golfers outdrive others who have more strength and weight.

Harry Vardon once said: "Golfers find it a very trying matter to turn at the waist, more particularly if they have a lot of waist to turn. But they must learn to do so if they would acquire any proficiency at all; it is the only way to success at golf."

A turn of the body is necessary, because there is no other way to get into position to hit the ball with power and force, yet with ease and rhythm. The pivot places the body behind the swing and gives freedom to the hands, wrists, and arms to do their part of the job. The turn of the body should be made naturally and comfortably, letting the hands swing fairly close to the body.

When the left shoulder drops and the golfer fails to complete the prior pivot, the right shoulder is swung too low in the downswing and the clubhead hits the ground. This fault can be traced to failure of the golfer to shift his weight to the right leg in the backswing.

The pivot isn't an artificial action; it is a natural turn of the body. Without holding a club, stand upright and turn the shoulders and hips from left to right and back again. This is simply the pivot action. Notice that in order to get the shoulders at right angles to the starting position, the left knee bends, and the left heel leaves the ground.

Straight Left Arm

A STRAIGHT LEFT ARM is not essential to good golf, but it is good form, and is conducive to a good game. Many fine golfers bend the left arm slightly at the top of the backswing, but early in the downswing, it is straightened so that at impact it is in a position that forms a straight line from the clubhead to the left shoulder.

Any excessive bend in the left arm destroys a feeling of power and force in the wrists. And don't forget, a straight left arm does not mean that it must be stiff; it should be only comfortably straight.

The left arm acts as a measuring stick to gauge correctly the distance to the ball. No measure can be accurately made unless the tape is tight — remember, a straight line is the shortest distance between two points, and not around a bent arm.

The left arm connects the club to the left shoulder, which is the hub of the swing. By keeping it straight, the swinging arc is lengthened, enabling the golfer to get a longer sweep at the ball.

One point to concentrate on is to see that the left arm is absolutely straight at impact. A bend at this position in the swing can only lead to heeling, topping, or missing the ball entirely, or to many other faults that result from the clubhead traveling beyond or inside the line of flight.

The extended left arm is also an aid to firmness, which is necessary in the swing.

The Follow Through and the Finish

THE FOLLOW THROUGH plays just as important a part in golf as it does in other sports. It results in an easy, rhythmical swing that is so all important to good golf. It is that part of the swing in which the clubhead travels for a few inches low and close to the ground after the ball is struck. If the player gives this part of the stroke a little thought, he will be aided in correctly executing those parts of the swing that precede it.

Maybe you are one of those golfers who say, "Why bother with that part of the swing that takes place after the ball is struck? Nothing can be done to alter the ball's flight after it has been sent on its way."

This is a fair question. It is answered by the following fact. By trying to make the clubhead follow out after the ball, the golfer will find that the hit has been from the inside. The left arm has stayed firm, and the hands have been kept in the correct path.

After the follow through takes place — but not before — the head may be raised. Now the player is ready for the finish of the stroke. The follow through continues with the right arm straight and the right knee bent. The body turns until the golfer faces the hole. At the finish, the right arm is fairly straight, and the wrists break. The finish should closely resemble the top of the backswing, but in reverse.

Timing

IT IS AN ODD FACT, but true, that no two golfers swing alike. This is remarkable, considering the number of fine professionals and amateurs. Yet all good golfers, through experience and practice, have developed timing suited to the movements of their individual swing. Timing is the co-ordination of all actions into one continuous, easy, flowing movement. This is the secret of the long accurate hitter.

To develop timing, the player must avoid tension and relax. The tighter the tension, the simpler it is to forget golf's basic fundamentals on which timing and rhythm of the swing depend.

A baseball pitcher cannot show his usual speed and control in throwing, if he jerks his arm back quickly. Whenever possible, he takes a slow, easy windup, and then puts his full power into the throw. Neither can the golfer control the club by quickly raising and lowering the clubhead. He must start slowly and gradually accelerate in the downswing so that the clubhead is traveling at its greatest speed at impact.

When you have reason to believe your timing is off, slow down the backstroke. Arrest the action at the start of the swing by pushing the club back slowly with the left hand. Do not pick it up in a hurry, tossing it over your shoulder.

Wait for the backswing to be completed before starting the club down, and avoid rushing the right shoulder around before the clubhead has reached the hitting area. Lead the club down with the left hand and arm so that the clubhead will be brought around on an inside arc.

Turning the body too quickly in the downswing can only result in a badly timed shot. This is called hitting too soon. Eagerness to hit hard is the common fault of the ordinary player. The experts delay the complete turn of the body toward the hole to allow the hands and arms to come through. Better control and distance will be obtained if the player will keep his body out of the swing until he wants the final punch, co-ordinating with the wrists, arms, and hands. However, don't be misled by thinking that the body stays out of the shot entirely. Good timing necessitates the natural turn of the body on both the backswing and the downswing.

Backswing

Start the club back with a push from the left side through the left hand and arm.

IF THE GOLFER wishes to achieve a certain amount of success and desires to lower his score, he should pay particular attention to the backswing. This highly important item will not take care of itself, as so many mediocre golfers think. These players wonder what is wrong when scores mount and shots go astray. It would be to their advantage to concentrate on executing a good backswing, and let the downswing take care of itself. Such thoughts as power needed in the downswing to make the ball travel a needed distance down the fairway should be excluded from their minds.

If the backswing is not properly performed, there can be little hope for a successful downswing. The player must be in a good position to accomplish the hitting part of the stroke.

Get set mentally before starting any motion. Think in terms of smoothness, excluding the desire to rush and hurry. Remember, one can, and should, spend twice as much time on the backswing as on the downswing.

After mental assurance is gained, the golfer should think of starting the club back with a push from the left side through the left hand and arm as the body turns. The club will be the last thing to move and will be dragged away from the ball, lagging behind the hands. This start will help toward a correct pivot. Allow the right hip to turn so that it will not block the hands and arms. The hips and shoulders should turn until the back of the player is presented to the hole.

Guard against breaking the wrists too quickly, for such action will hinder the success of the pivot and the top of the swing will be reached before the pivot is completed. Let the wrists be cocked when the upper part of the backswing is reached. If the player will start the club back low and close to the ground, controlled by the left hand, breaking of the wrists too soon will be avoided.

Action of Hands and Arms

THE LEFT HAND is responsible for maintaining the correct position of the clubhead throughout the swing. Therefore, a secure grip must be maintained at all times. But golf is not just a left-handed game. The right also should have a reasonably secure hold on the club, for it plays its part in the downswing when it whips the club through the hitting region.

The right hand must not be allowed to overpower the left, for an overpowering right hand turns the clubface out of position, often cutting across the line of flight. Let the left hand and arm dominate the backswing and the downswing.

Do not grip too fiercely. The grip must be firm, but when the fingers grip too tightly, tension may spread to all parts of the body. Tight fingers cause the muscles of the arms to tighten. This is bound to result in a jerky swing.

To loosen the muscles of the hands and forearms, a waggle is recommended. A practice swing is also a good way to get properly set for the swing.

Instructors advise their pupils to start the downswing slowly. The reason for this is to guard against the arms swinging too swiftly toward the objective. Such action causes one to force or press the shot. When the golfer begins to press, the arms are traveling so fast the body cannot keep pace. Thus the stroke is made with the arms alone, and power is lost. Speed of the arms should be gradually increased. The climax comes with the forward snap of the wrists.

Analyze

Your Grip

"V's" formed should point over the right shoulder.

WHETHER THE GOLFER uses the interlocking, the old-fashioned baseball, or the popular overlapping or Vardon grip, the left hand should be turned over the shaft. Analyzing the grip will show that this assists one in keeping a straight left arm by slightly increasing the tension of the left elbow, preventing it from crumbling at impact.

A firmer grip on the club is advised by the experts for iron play. It is necessary to carry the clubhead through. Don't confuse this with tightening of the wrists. This must be avoided at all times.

In a sand trap or heavy rough, the firm grip is of utmost importance, for it is sometimes necessary literally to plow through the grass or sand to get the ball out. Grasp the club firmly enough so that any obstruction will not turn the club in your hands. If this happens, the clubface will be presented to the ball at an incorrect angle.

While on the subject of the grip, let me warn you about the right hand. Faulty placement of it can be the direct cause for the quick-diving smothered shot, or the hooked iron. When the right hand is placed too far under the shaft, a rolling action of the wrists takes place, which results in turning the right hand over the left. This closes the face of the clubhead or hoods the club just before impact, resulting in the diving hook.

Practice

THE PRACTICE TEE is the place to make corrections. Even professionals practice as much as they play. Experimenting when the chips are down might be disastrous.

But if you find your No. 5 iron is not working properly, do not rush to the practice tee and begin hitting No. 5 iron shots. First get the advice of your pro, find the fault, and then proceed to correct it. Just hitting shots, hoping the stroke will correct itself, is useless. You then are inclined to repeat the error over and over again.

It is a good idea to practice before a round of golf. A fifteen-minute warmup will help your game considerably. But do not practice with one club too long, for when interest wanes, practice is useless. The player then gets careless with the stroke and often bad hits are formed.

Practice loosens muscles that have been more or less idle and which will be used during a round. Arm, shoulder, and back muscles are called on to do work to which they are unaccustomed. Practice loosens the wrists, the action of which is essential to good golf.

Start practice by hitting a few putts. Then work up to the longer clubs.

A fine way to start practice with the irons is to start pitching at a distance of about twenty-five yards from the green. If, after a dozen shots, you are satisfied with the results, move back another twenty-five yards. If this stroke also clicks move back another twenty-five yards, and so on. In this manner you are bound to find the spot at which your shots may not be working so well, and so be able to correct your swing. This method also gradually loosens the muscles used in the longer strokes without putting them to too great a strain at once.

Causes for
Topped Shots

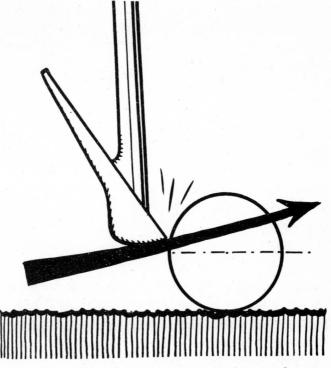

Topped shot results when ascending clubhead hits ball above center.

TOPPING A SHOT is aggravating, and one topped shot is apt to ruin the complacency and rhythm of all but the most composed golfers.

This annoying accident is mainly caused by the golfer trying to lift the ball into the air with a body action, or by a flick of the wrists. When the golfer tries to get the ball into the air in this manner, he fails to shift the weight onto the left leg, keeps too much on the right, and the result is that the lowest point in the swinging arc is moved backward.

A topped ball is seldom hit on top, as the duffer imagines. It actually is hit above center after the clubhead has reached the lowest point in the downswing and has begun to ascend.

Another cause for a topped shot is looking up or lifting the head before impact. This action draws the clubhead out of its intended path. Also responsible for a "top," is a failure to pivot. This fault lets the right shoulder drop in the downswing. When this happens, the chances are that the clubhead will hit the ground before the ball is topped. Still another cause for this annoyance is the tendency to play the ball too far advanced. It then can only be hit an upward blow, and you will be lucky if the ball is hit cleanly if played from such a position.

Learn the fundamentals of the swing, practice them diligently, and your topping will stop.

Line of flight.

Causes of Slicing

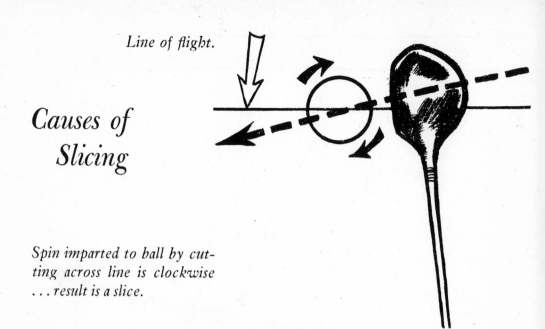

Spin imparted to ball by cutting across line is clockwise ... result is a slice.

EXPERTS SELDOM SLICE, because their swing has been built with the idea of hooking the ball. The average golfer, however, still in the early stages of building his game, finds the slice a troubling factor, and is bewildered and helpless when it comes to correcting it.

Many faults can creep into the swing to cause the ball to be hit in a disgusting, though graceful arc into the rough to the right of the fairway. The main reason however is that the face of the clubhead has been drawn across the ball. This means that the clubhead has been caused to travel in a path that cuts across the line of flight from the outside.

But one must go farther back in the swing to find the sources for this cut across the ball. Too wide a stance is one. Lack of proper control by the left hand is another. When the left hand quits, there is no guiding factor to hold the clubhead along the line of flight, and it is drawn sharply in toward the left side.

Chronic slicers get the hands and body into the stroke too soon. In their anxiety to hit, the hands and body lead the clubhead at impact. When the clubhead is allowed to drag behind, the clubface strikes the ball while at a distinct angle, with the heel ahead of the toe or with an open face.

A similar position of the clubface may be traced to the bend or collapse of the left arm or the lack of wrist snap, at or just before impact.

If slicing is to be cured, check on these points: see that the clubhead is started back inside the line; that the left side is completing the turn, with the weight shifted against the right leg; that the left hand and arm are dominating the backswing and the start of the downswing; and that the stance is not that for the intentional slice which hinders a complete pivot.

Playing in the Wind

THERE ARE FEW PLAYERS who enjoy a round of golf on a windy day. Wind not only affects the flight of the ball, but plays havoc with the player's morale.

The ball must be more accurately hit when playing in a gale; therefore the first thing to do is shorten the backswing and hit less viciously. A shorter swing is more compact, affords the player better balance, and he is less likely to err. Do not fight the wind. It is an invisible, unbeatable opponent.

Wind magnifies mistakes, and shots that would look as if perfectly played on a calm day, are completely carried away.

A low trajectory shot is the one desired in iron play. Use a club with less loft, and play a half-iron shot. The ball will be lower and, although it may run more than a highly hit approach, direction, the thing to be achieved, is the result.

Try teeing the ball a little lower for the wood shots. Through the fairway, when the lie is good, a driver often should be the club selected in preference to the brassie.

If the wind is blowing from left to right, don't aggravate a condition by allowing for the wind to swing the ball back to the middle of the fairway. The golfer then unconsciously assumes a stance of that for the intentional slice. A ball hit in this manner slices more than ever. The idea is to play for a slight draw. This can be accomplished by turning the left wrist more over the shaft, or closing the stance slightly so that the hit from the inside is accentuated. The reverse holds true if the wind is blowing from right to left. Open the stance and hit with the clubhead slightly open.

When shooting directly into the wind off the tee, many golfers employ what is known as the "knock down shot." They play the ball more toward the right foot and connect with a descending stroke. This shot has a low start, a quick rise, and, due to the backspin, stops almost instantly upon striking the ground. It is a good one to use for second shots to the green, but has little value as a distance-getter. The best distance-getter is the ball, whether playing in the wind or not, that is struck squarely in the back. Let it take its normal trajectory and you will find it a better boring ball than one hit in the other manner.

Top of the Backswing

A pause at the top of the backswing will check the desire to kill the ball.

IF THE ACTIONS of the backstroke have been made correctly, the golfer will feel a pull at the left shoulder with the right arm and shoulder relaxed. The left side will be taut, for it will start the action back toward the ball.

If the right side is in control here, there is an irresistible desire to hit from this position, with a tendency to turn the shoulders as soon as the downswing is started. Therefore, be sure control is in the left hand.

Here the greater portion of the weight should have been shifted to the right foot. If it has not, the backswing has been checked and is working against a resisting force. The shoulders then cannot swing around, and the hips bend in a sideward action to the left rather than turning in a rotating manner toward the right.

At the top of the backswing, the grip on the shaft must be firm. Often golfers open the hands here, with the result that the grip is altered in the downswing. Then when contact with the ball is made, the grip is not the same as it was at address.

Studying the Putt

THE PUTTER is probably the most neglected club in the bag. It is hard to make the golfer realize the value of the putt. He figures that par allows him 36 putts on the carpet, and any figure in that vicinity is satisfactory and good putting. It isn't good putting and shouldn't be satisfactory to any golfer. It is on the greens that the golfer should give Old Man Par a licking.

If the player is to improve in this department, there are things he should do besides executing the fundamentals described elsewhere on these pages. Mental condition has a great bearing on results. Worries over a past score, a business deal back in town, or other personal problems will be of no help. These worries will affect putting more than any other part of the game. This is the delicate part of the game, and a cool head is mandatory. Put all thoughts out of your mind but that one of sending the ball to the bottom of the cup.

There are also things the golfer should do before he addresses the ball. He should study the green, surveying the line to the hole. Determine the roll of the green. Study the grass, noting whether it grows in a certain way; that is, if the blades all seem to lean in one direction. They will have a decided effect on the path of the ball, pushing it in the direction they are leaning. This is important when playing a rolling green. Against the grass grain, the golfer should allow less burrow. With the grain, the ball will break quicker. Putting against the grain requires a harder tap than putting with it.

The Importance of a Proper Stance

THE STANCE is the foundation of the swing, but the foundation will crumble and along with it the golfer's game if the placement of the feet is made improperly. Therefore, it is an all-important factor to check the foundation and see that it is in line and that its parts are in the proper place.

The proper stance has the knees slightly bent so that relaxation throughout the swing is maintained. Toes point outward so that tension in the legs is avoided. The feet should not be placed too far apart. Pivoting will then be difficult. It is much easier to complete the pivot if the feet are closer together.

With a wide stance, instead of pivoting naturally, the player is bound to sway in an effort to complete the backswing. It is then impossible to get the body into the stroke, and a shorter shot results. A narrower stance enables the player to impart considerable acceleration to the clubhead with the body turn alone.

Golfers speak of three kinds of stances. The square is the most popular. It has the toes lined up evenly with the line of flight. The open stance, used by many golfers when playing iron shots, has the left foot drawn away from the line of flight. It is a good stance to use when one is over-swinging. The closed stance has the right foot drawn back from the line, and is often used by the golfer who finds it difficult to pivot. It is the stance taken to play the intentional hook.

Whichever stance is used, be sure it is suited to your swing.

Wrists at Top of Swing

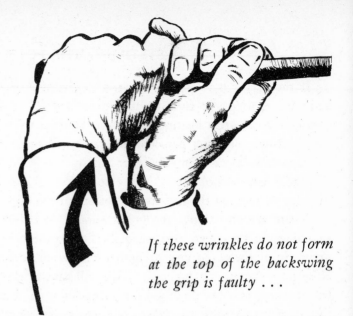

If these wrinkles do not form at the top of the backswing the grip is faulty . . .

POWER IN THE WRISTS puts power in the golfer's swing, and the cocking of them in the backswing imparts speed and power in the downswing when they are un-cocked. If the wrists are not cocked at the top of the swing, the golfer depends on his speed and power to come from the body, and exerts a tremendous effort to attain only a portion of the efficiency attainable in the swing. Without the wrists being cocked, the golfer is very likely to press his swing.

Power behind a carpenter's hammer comes from cocking the wrists, and not from the muscles of his arm. Try swinging a hammer without a cock of the wrist, and note the lack of power in the blow.

Wrists are the hinges of the golf swing, connecting the hands and club with the arms and body. They must work with freedom and ease, and not like the rusty hinge that squeaks and complains under any action. Well-oiled and free, the hinge works smoothly. Avoid a vise-like grip; a firm but easy one frees the wrists of tension. If the wrists lack freedom and ease, the player attempts to make up the loss of power by quickly lunging at the ball in the downswing.

To achieve distance off the tee, it is imperative that the wrists should be cocked and in the correct position at the top of the backswing. Here there should be a distinct bend in the left wrist, so that the hand points inward toward the right shoulder, with the right wrist almost vertical under the shaft.

The golfer might check to see that wrinkles are formed just below the thumb and index finger of the left hand. The grip is faulty if the wrinkles do not appear. The hands have been placed too far under the shaft in gripping at address.

With this imperfection it is impossible to derive maximum power from the wrists, for the hit will be but a backhanded slap by the left wrist. More power is secured by hitting sideways — another reason why the left hand should be turned more over the shaft than under; in other words, good wrist action at the top of the backswing depends on the correct grip.

Side Hill Lies

THERE ARE NO OTHER SHOTS in golf that will test the player's skill more than abnormal lies. Side hill lies are bugaboos, and the golfer should know how to play them, for all shots off the fairway are not from level ground.

The golfer often goes about playing from this lie with the idea that, being handicapped, he must give it a bit more effort; rather, he should bear in mind that the stroke should be made with less effort than he is wont to give.

As when playing in a wind, the golfer is tempted to add a bit more power to the stroke and probably presses as a result. The more difficult the lie, the more easily the golfer should go about recovery.

When playing a side hill lie in which the ball rests on the ground in a higher position than the feet, the feeling is always one of cramped conditions. To correct this, the swing is restricted. You have to grip the club a little lower, therefore the arc of swing is shorter. The club feels lighter and a quicker swing is the result. Careful timing of this shot is essential. Guard against falling away from the shot. Keep your head down.

When the ball is lower than the feet, one gets the feeling that the club is too short, and the player may find himself reaching for the ball. Keep the arc of the swing within its limits, and again watch your turning.

Quick Cure for Hooking and Slicing

TWO OF THE MAIN DEFECTS in his game which a golfer should know how to correct quickly are hooking and slicing, those bugaboos which put the player in more hot water and into more difficult lies than probably any other department of the game.

To make the correction, the golfer first must know the cause. Spin is the factor that produces a hooked or sliced shot, and this is imparted to the ball by the clubhead cutting across the ball. A hook is produced by hitting the ball from inside the line of flight out; a slice results from hitting from outside the line of flight in.

Of the two aggravations, slicing is the most common in the swing of the average golfer. One of the most common reasons for a sliced shot is that, when on the tee, determined to avoid a slice, the player will generally try to yank the shot to the left of the fairway. This results in the clubhead being pulled in, cutting across the ball and imparting a slice spin.

Here's how to go about curing your slice — first check the rudiments of your swing, making sure your grip is correct and that your stance is not for the intentional slice, which has the left foot drawn back from the line of flight, which is purposely used to get around obstacles between the golfer and green on occasions. Now attempt to hit the ball to the right of the fairway. This will aid in bringing the clubhead in to the ball more from the inside.

When the player runs into a period of hooking, the hit from the inside has been amplified. The left hand no doubt is throwing the club away from the body and the right elbow is too far from the side of the body in the downswing. This, of course, does not apply to the badly-smothered diving hook that quickly scampers into the rough. This is caused by the hands rolling over, or the right shoulder being higher than the left at impact.

A quick cure for the hook is the reverse action to that which is used to cure a slice — try to hit to the left of the fairway.

The Cut Shot

To stop the ball quickly when playing a shot of 50 yards or less, lay the face of the niblick back.

THE CUT SHOT is one that saves any golfer many strokes. It is used in a situation where the ball needs extraction from heavy grass, or from a trap. Often it is used to pitch the ball onto the green when it is necessary to make the ball stop quickly.

When the normal loft of the club is not sufficient to make the ball rise quickly, this is the shot to use.

Successfully to play this shot out of a sand trap, the ball should be played off the left foot with an open stance. The body should almost be facing the hole.

The club should be laid well back and taken outside the line of flight, cutting across the line in the downswing. Objective of the golfer should be to cut under the ball, slicing a thin cushion of sand between it and the clubhead. Supple wrists are necessary here, as the shot calls for plenty of wrist action.

Here you should be able to differentiate between force and effort. Enough force should be used to cause the club to bite through the sand, but it is not a shot that requires an enormous amount of effort. The moment you think of exerting too much effort, you immediately eliminate the naturalness that should accompany the shot. When the player tries to give the shot all he has — and often more than he has — the backswing is hurried, and a quick lunge at the ball results in an inaccurate, ill-timed blow.

When playing the shot off solid ground, often in a grassy lie, the ball is played more toward the right foot with an open stance. Be sure to hit the ball first, taking a bit of turf with the clubhead after it has made contact with the ball.

Value of Good Form

ONE CAN SOON REALIZE the value of good form if he will take a moment to study its meaning. Good form is the co-ordination of all parts of the swing into continuous rhythmic movement. It cannot be imitated; it must be achieved by constant practice.

Some players attain a certain amount of success without good form, but all good golfers have it. Their styles may vary, but they all have form.

Webster's dictionary defines "form" as "appearance to the eye." If something looks good, it has good form. If a player's swing looks good, he has good form, and you can be sure he has executed the different parts of the swing correctly. Another Webster definition says: "to model by instruction and discipline." Therefore, if the player has learned the fundamentals of the swing from instruction, and if he disciplines his mind to execute them correctly, he cannot help but reach his goal, *Good Form.*

If the swing is to look good, the player must be able to do the thing he wants to in a free and easy manner without strain or tension. Bobby Jones once said, "Good form simply is the means of eliminating waste motion and of exerting, in a useful way, a greater portion of the physical strength which the player possesses."

Trap Shots

Let club enter sand about an inch behind ball.

Low SCORES are made by saving strokes, and the average player wastes more of them in a trap than any other place on the course. To him, a trip into a bunker is a harrowing experience.

When in a trap, it is important that the player have a proper coordination of mind, muscles, and nerves. This controls perfect timing.

There are four ways of extracting a ball from the sand. They are dependent on the lie, how far the ball is from the pin, whether the sand is wet or dry, how far the ball should be hit, and how much sand it is required to take.

The explosion shot is the safest way out of a bunker. The stance must be firm — so wiggle the feet in the sand until you are well set. The shot is played off the left foot. Stand fairly erect and try a fairly upright swing, brought rather sharply down, driving the clubhead on through just beneath the ball. Let the clubhead enter the sand a few inches behind the ball. In other words, try to hit the sand under the ball, forcing it against the bottom of the ball rather than hitting behind the ball. The latter action drives the sand against the side, circumventing your desire to loft the ball. Properly executed, a quick loft is assured and you will be out in one stroke.

Range can be determined by the amount of sand taken. If it is dry and loose, the hit behind the ball can be farther than if the sand is wet and heavy. Don't let the clubhead strike the ball; the force of the sand under the ball will send it out.

Another factor to be sure of is to follow through, and not to let the club quit and stay buried in the sand. You need not fear knocking the ball too far if enough sand is taken.

The cut shot has been explained elsewhere. It is a delicate shot to play out of traps, and one that requires considerable practice.

The chip shot can be employed if the lie is favorable and the ball is not buried. The ball must be hit cleanly. Do not attempt to use this stroke if the bank is steep and the top is covered with overhanging grass.

The putter can also be used to good effect if the trap is shallow.

One of the most common faults of the golfer who finds himself in a bunker is to look up too soon as he makes his recovery shot. Keep the head down and the body relaxed.

If the lie in the trap is good and distance is needed, the shot is played the same as from the fairway. But don't ground the club — it's against the rules.

Backspin or English

THERE ARE TIMES in a round of golf when it is necessary to impart English, or backspin, to the ball so that when it hits the green it will come to a quick stop.

Hitting a shot with backspin is an easy matter if the golfer will get one fact firmly in mind — the ball must be hit a downward blow and be struck before the clubhead bites into the turf.

A backspin shot is not made with a wide stance; rather, it is made with one that is open, heels just a few inches apart. The ball is played off the right foot.

Remembering that your shot must leave the ball nearly dead on the green — keep the left arm straight through the stroke — go into the shot with determination. If correctly made, the hands will finish out in front pointing toward the objective. The length of the backswing varies according to the distance to be carried.

Backspin is not only used when pitching, but is also of great value when correctly applied to the chip shot. When used for chipping, backspin is applied by pinching the ball between the clubface and the ground at impact. This will make the ball take off quickly and travel in a low arc. You may think it has been hit too hard, but watch how it pulls up after hitting the green. It seems to have brakes.

A ball with backspin bores its way and holds its line. That is why experts rely on backspin for accuracy even in high wind.

125

In connection with backspin, the golfer should know how to apply what is known as "fade" to the ball so that when an opening presents itself to the left of the green he can make the ball travel in from that side. This is done by assuming an open stance and cutting across the intended line of flight as the clubhead comes into the ball.

Recovery Shots

TAKE INVENTORY on the shots wasted in a round, and note how many were caused by failing to recover correctly. The recovery should be made with only one stroke. In other words, when a shot has gone astray, be sure to select a club that will get you out in one stroke and execute it so that no more are needed to get out of trouble.

A little attention and correct thinking can save the golfer from five to ten strokes in a trip around the course. Don't gamble three strokes trying to save one.

Average golfers do not like to practice recovery shots. Seldom do you see any practice from heavy rough, or from a sand trap. Remember, to be able to recover from a bad spot is just as important as avoiding the error that put you there in the first place.

The same distance cannot be made from heavy rough that can be made from a clean lie in the fairway. It is foolish to shoot for the green when it is impossible to reach it. It is better to pitch to the fairway and play the ball from there.

There is little reason for using the cut shot when the maximum distance is required. The cut shot floats in the air, and is used only for short recoveries. To obtain length out of the rough, play the ball more off the right foot and hit with an upright arc, bringing the clubhead down sharply on the ball. No attempt should be made to hit the ball with a sweeping blow, for the long grass will slow up the clubhead.

Sometimes a golfer's sporting blood will entice him to try a shot out of water. It has been done, and is similarly played to the explosion from sand. However, the chances are against you unless part of the ball is lying above the surface of the water. Water bends light rays at crazy angles, and if the ball is completely covered, and fairly deep, it may be a few inches from the spot at which you are looking. When in water, it is safer to take the one-stroke penalty and drop behind the hazard.

Lawson Little once took twelve strokes to recover from water when playing in the Greater Greensboro, N. C. Open of 1938. Ray Ainsley, during the National Open at Cherry Hills, Denver, in 1939, amassed the total of nineteen for a par 4 hole by attempting to play a ball out of water.

The Right Arm and Elbow

Keep right arm and elbow close to side.

To INSURE CONTROL at the top of the backswing, the right elbow must not be allowed to wander too far from the right side. Never should the arm be lifted higher than the shoulder. When it is, the golfer can look for a faulty pivot. If the turn of the body has not been completed, it is impossible to get the club to the horizontal position in the backswing without committing this error.

When this fault takes place, the golfer can be sure that the right hand has played too great a part in the backward movement, and you can look for it to dominate the downswing by hitting as soon as the forward stroke gets under way. A hook or a badly smothered shot can easily result.

When the right arm is kept close, the right hand will not overpower the left.

Discard Wooden Tee on Short Holes

SINCE TURF should be taken when playing an iron shot, it is far better to play from a favorable spot on the teeing surface rather than set the ball up on a wooden peg.

In iron play, the ball must be hit a downward blow; therefore turf must be taken and backspin applied to be accurate. If the ball is teed, it is almost impossible to take turf. The ball slides off the clubface and less backspin is applied than when the ball is pinched between the turf and the clubface.

If a raised ball gives you more confidence, do as other players do — flick up a bit of earth with the toe of the clubhead and rest the ball on top of that.

Speed of Clubhead

*The left arm and club form
a straight line at impact.*

THE LENGTH of a drive depends on the speed of the clubhead. The faster it travels, the farther the ball travels.

The clubhead should be swung as rapidly as is accurately possible, and speed is dependent on correct wrist action.

Most golfers hit too soon; that is, they begin the uncoiling of the wrists long before the hands have moved two-thirds of the way down from the top position. Hitting force then has been expended before the clubhead reaches the ball.

From the cocked position at the top of the backswing, the wrists remain in the same relation to the shaft of the club until half-way through the downswing. Here is little change, except that the forward wrist action of the right hand, which until now has stayed out of the swing, takes place. The hands may then travel only a few inches while the clubhead moves three feet or more. The clubhead now is reaching the maximum speed as the right hand snaps it through the ball.

Viewed from in front of the player, the correct action of the wrists brings the shaft of the club and the left arm in a straight line at impact.

Difference in Wood
and Iron Strokes

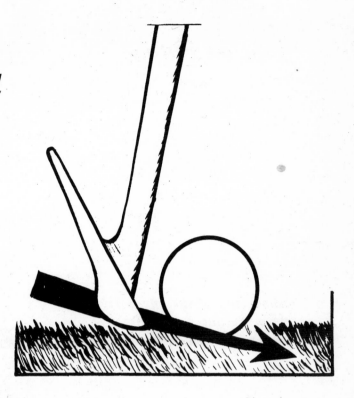

*In iron play hit the ball
a downward blow . . .*

FEW GOLFERS who score over 100 for a round realize that there is a distinct difference in the wood shot and that with the iron. They go their merry way swinging both clubs alike.

The arc of the swing in wood play is longer than for the iron. It is essentially a sweep, and has more follow through than that of the iron. It makes less contact with the ground.

Accuracy, not distance, is the aim when playing an iron; hence a shorter backswing. The abbreviated swing requires less pivot, and the stroke is more of a punch or a distinct hit.

The downswing of both strokes is much the same up until the time of contact with the ball. Just before reaching the lowest point in the arc of the downswing, the iron meets the ball in a crisp descending blow, then tears into the turf. In the wood shot, the ball is struck while the clubhead is at the lowest point in the downswing, hitting the ball a sweeping blow.

Tips on Putting

Allow the wrists to work when putting . . . stiffness must be avoided.

TENSION IS A FACTOR that can cause the player to have a bad day on the putting surface. If the muscles of the forearm tighten, the ball is stabbed with a stiff, jerky swing, instead of a free, pendulum action. Allow the wrists to have freedom by loosening the grip on the club.

As in other golf strokes, swaying should be avoided. A player who keeps his body still during the putting stroke, stands a better chance of becoming a good putter than one who lets it move back and forth with the action of the clubhead.

Stroke hard enough to reach the hole. You have heard the old adage, "never up, never in." Always play to sink the ball with the first putt. It is better to overrun than fall short. When direction is good the putt that has been hit too hard may hit the back of the cup and drop in. The putt played short requires another stroke.

Here are three suggestions that will aid the mediocre putter. Stand close to the ball, with a greater portion of the weight on the left foot. The duffer stands too far from the ball, losing control and direction. Don't grip too tightly. It stiffens the muscles and prevents relaxation. Swing the putter slowly and smoothly. Do not jab at the ball as if in a hurry to get the stroke over.

Keep the putter at right angles to the line.

Chip and Run-up Shots

THE CHIP SHOT is an exaggerated putt played with a more lofted club, such as a No. 3, 4, or 5 iron, or a club with even greater loft, as necessity arises.

The ball should be played far enough from the body so that the clubhead is not resting on its toe, yet close enough so that it is not resting on the heel. In other words, allow the clubhead to rest flush on the turf so that there will be no turning of the clubface in either direction as the ball is struck.

As in putting, take a comfortable position. Do not crouch over the ball or keep the feet far apart. An upright position, with the ball opposite the left heel, is much easier. Swing the clubhead low and close to the ground in the backstroke and the follow through. Swing more uprightly when a more lofted shot is necessary.

When playing the run-up shot, the ball should be played so that it will fall short of the putting surface and then roll to the hole. The ball is played back farther and the stroke is lightly downward. No pivot is required. The arms should be kept close to the sides, and only wrist and forearms used to make the swing. Of course, the length of the backswing varies according to the distance from the green.

The Left Heel

Do not consciously lift the left heel when playing a pitch shot.

THERE ARE DIFFERENT SCHOOLS OF THOUGHT on whether the left heel should be lifted in the backswing for the pitch shot. It is a question often debated in the locker rooms by leading golf professionals. Some golfers argue that it is better to keep both heels on the ground and let the hands and arms do the work.

A notable feature of Gene Sarazen's method of playing the pitch shot is that he uses little ankle and knee action, though he uses a free turn of the body from the hips up. He keeps the left heel on the ground.

Lifting of the left heel in the backswing should never be consciously done. It is the turning of the hips that causes the left knee to bend sufficiently to lift the left heel from the ground. Being mindful that the left heel must be lifted often causes the golfer to sway. Swaying must be avoided if the iron shot is to be a compact one.

In short approaches, where less hip action is required, the knee action at times is not enough to lift the heel from the ground. However, if the body-turn is sufficient to lift the heel, don't get the idea that you are executing the backswing for the pitch shot incorrectly. George Duncan, a great British golfer in his day, lifted the left heel, as did MacDonald Smith, one of the finest stylists the game has ever produced.

Impact

AT IMPACT, the position of the hands and arms should be similar to that at address.

Here the left arm should be firm, guiding the club through and maintaining the radius of the swing. The left hand has been in control of the swing up until now, but just before impact and thereafter, the right takes over, hitting against the left as the clubhead nears the ball. This snap of the wrists accelerates the speed of the clubhead, adding yardage to the drive.

The correct swing has the shoulders about parallel to the line of flight, with the right shoulder under the left.

Guard against getting the right side around too quickly, for body action will be wasted and the clubhead will be drawn across the ball. Also beware of putting your body action into the swing too late. The hips should be thrust forward, and the left leg straightened to brace the body as the arms swing the clubhead down against the ball. At this stage, both arms are straight, as the wrists and forearms do their part in speeding the clubhead through.

The left arm must not be allowed to collapse against the left side, for in a bent position, it cannot possibly swing the club out along the line of flight.

Shanking Avoided

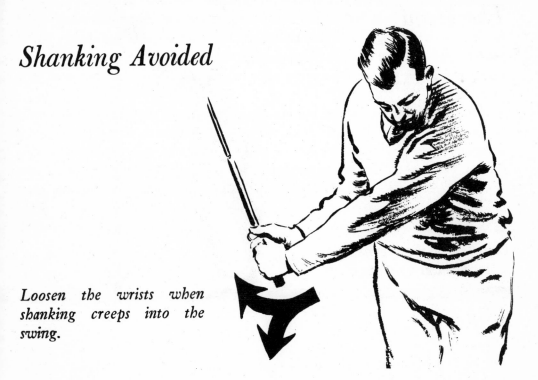

Loosen the wrists when shanking creeps into the swing.

To my mind, the most disgusting and uncalled for shot in golf is that which is made by striking the ball with the neck or that part of the clubhead that bends into the shaft. It is commonly known as shanking or socketing.

Causes for this type of annoyance can be found in a hurried backswing, followed by a hurried downswing, which throws the hands and clubhead out beyond their correct paths.

Forcing the shot is another reason. This is because the golfer tries to make a number 5 iron do the work of a number 4. It will cause the golfer to be over-anxious to hit. This form of pressing can only result in a shanked shot.

Quitting on the shot, or attempting a stroke with no freedom of the wrists, is still another cause. Lack of wrist action will cause the clubhead to travel outside the line of flight. When wrists are locked, the golfer often attempts to make up lost power by a sway or lunge of the body toward the ball.

To avoid this demoralizing stroke, loosen up the wrists. Keep the hands close to the body. Some of the better golfers keep the hands so close that at times they brush their trouser legs.

The Head

Experts keep the eyes on spot where ball was teed long after impact.

THE HEAD is often referred to as the anchor of the golf swing. It keeps the club-head in its correct path.

You may argue that you have seen expert golfers move the head during the swing, and you are partially right. Fast action pictures have shown that good shot makers do move the head — but it is a slight movement, and it is a good idea to keep the head as close to the address position as possible all during the stroke. It is one way of acquiring a grooved swing.

Think of the head as the axle of a wheel, the club as a spoke, and the club-head as part of the rim. Any movement of the axle is transferred to the rim through the spoke. If the head, or axle, is lifted, control of the clubhead, or rim, is lost. Experts keep the head in the same position for some time after the ball is struck.

The head should not be held so rigidly that tension welds it to the top of the body. This is as bad a condition as moving the head during the swing. If the head is completely isolated from the rest of the body through rigidity, turning of the shoulders cannot take place in a proper swing.

When tension appears, and the head begins to pop up before the ball is struck, attempt to execute the stroke with more ease, starting the swing more slowly. Check the grip; tension might have started there.

The Hitting Region

Wrists stay cocked until hands have dropped below level of waist.

THE HITTING REGION is that part of the swing, just before impact, where the uncocking of the wrists takes place, adding speed to the clubhead. Through this part of the swing the clubhead travels at its maximum speed, faster and many times farther in relation to the hands.

Many golfers uncock their wrists too soon in the downswing, spending punch and power long before the club is in position to hit. When this takes places, one can be sure the right hand has assumed control at the start of the downswing.

The wrists should stay cocked until the hands have dropped below the waist and should not begin to unwind until the club is parallel to the ground.

At the start of the hitting region, the right arm has just started its straightening action, but the elbow is still bent and hugging the right side. It might be said that through the hitting region and not before is where the right hand comes into the stroke, whipping the clubhead through.

As already stated, if the wrists uncoil too soon, power is lost; if they are late in whipping the clubhead through, the clubface will hit the ball at an angle which will result in a pushed shot.

The Mental Side

How MANY TIMES have you started the season, or, after a long layoff from the game, resumed golfing by shooting a score that was better than expected? Shortly after, however, you find your score mounting. A good score early in the season can be attributed to the correct mental attitude. Your first "surprise" round probably was played completely relaxed and with the thought in mind that a score quite a few strokes above normal would be satisfactory.

Following this initial round, the golfer is bound to make a few bad shots. Then when he finds he is not quite sure of himself, he wonders what may have taken place to add a few bad ones to his score. His total mounts, and he begins to seek a cure for the trouble.

He takes inventory of his knowledge of the game and tries to remember all the "do's" and "don'ts" he has read and been told about. He reviews his swing. He contemplates his form. In desperation, he seeks the advice of his playing partner or pro, lamenting that he hasn't the faintest idea as to what he is doing wrong.

There is no player who can make a good golf stroke without giving a bit of thought to the action. So how can a player in such a state of mind think of the simplest fundamentals? With thoughts of that trap in front that must be carried crowding his mind, his head pops up long before the clubhead approaches the ball in the downswing. The result need not be mentioned. This player has listened to advice, but it has failed to penetrate a befuddled mind.

Let the player concentrate on but one thought in the swing — your pro or partner will tell you where you're off. If this is not the cure, select another suspected fault, concentrating on that point until the swing is working normally again.

Often golfers, in trying to cure one fault, exaggerate another. Suppose your body action is a bit faulty. You change the placement of your hands, forgetting the grip that stood you in good stead in the past. Now you have acquired another fault. In a desperate effort to affect a cure, you have added a third error.

Being mentally upset, the golfer has allowed tension to creep into the swing. To eliminate this tension, check and see that three points are relaxed. The wrists, the muscles controling the shoulders, and those in control of the lower part of the torso. If they are working freely, your shots will soon straighten out. By all means do not worry about a few badly-hit shots. Eliminate the thought of them from your mind, and concentrate on the shot at hand.

Balance

*Settle well back on the heels
at address.*

AN IMPORTANT but often-neglected item in the golf swing is the matter of balance. Many golfers rise on their toes at the moment of impact. It is impossible to do this and maintain balance. Watch these golfers and you will note that they take a step forward with the right foot soon after the ball is struck. This is proof that they lacked balance throughout the swing, and that it was necessary to take this step to keep from falling over.

Only one heel should leave the ground at a time in the swing. Naturally it is the left in the backswing and the right in the downswing.

Do not reach for the ball, so that the weight will be pulled to the toes at address. It is better to settle well back on the heels where the golfer will find himself in a more comfortable position for the backstroke and the downswing. This also produces relaxation and banishes tension.

If you have the opportunity to watch star performers, you will see that the right heel is firm on the ground during the backswing, and the left is well anchored at the moment of impact.

Getting the Ball Into the Air

FAILURE TO GET THE BALL INTO THE AIR is a common fault of the beginner. It is hard to convince him that he should let the clubhead do the work. Often he keeps putting the ball closer and closer to the hole – playing it more off the left foot – at address, with the thought in mind that he has to boost the ball up in the air instead of allowing the loft on the face of the club to produce the desired elevation. He is surprised when advised to play the ball farther back – more off the right foot – and hit down on it.

Few golfers realize the important part backspin plays in getting the ball up. It is not only the loft of the clubhead that makes the ball climb – when the golfer depends only on the loft of the club to raise the ball, the trajectory will be considerably lower than if he hits down on it, imparting spin. Backspin sends the ball into the air because of the tendency of this spin to cause it to rise against air resistance, and the more loft to the club, the more backspin can be applied.

The swing should be more upright with less pivot. The clubhead is brought down more abruptly than when playing a wood, where the stroke should be a long sweep at the ball.

How Pros Correct Their Faults

DON'T GET THE IDEA that all golf professionals are perfect-game robots, and that they never make mistakes. Remember, to err is human, even with the pros. Some top-notch experts have natural faults which they must constantly guard against. A certain National Open Champion may have this fault corrected by now, but not so long ago he told me that all his life his leading fault was a closed face. He overcomes this error in his swing by placing the right hand more on top of the shaft, with the club well in the fingers, and accentuating the left hand pronation.

A Ryder Cupper says a fault he must watch out for is hooking. The way he corrects it is to see that, in making the backswing, his body turns with the club instead of picking the club up. And he keeps his feet anchored. He claims that with this move working correctly, it gives him sufficient leverage to make the downswing without throwing the club from the top.

"This is the worst fault of the average golfer," he says. "They try to hit, instead of swing."

"You have to get the right position at the top of the backswing. If you do not arrive at this position, it makes the player swing very fast and throws the body and club out of time."

The average golfer making this move incorrectly has more or less a tendency to slice, but the good players, who use their hands well, naturally hook the ball.

A former National Open winner tells me the biggest trouble he has encountered over a period of time is the shortening of his backswing entirely too much. Being characteristically an abbreviated swinger, his backstroke became shorter and shorter, especially if he laid off competition for any length of time. As he shortened the backswing, the face of the club closed to such an extent that it caused hooking. He remedied this mistake by lengthening the backswing to a point where the club reached at least the horizontal position. A very good way of doing this, he says, is to watch for the clubhead out of the corner of the left eye. Of course, this should be done in practice until it becomes automatic and one loses the self-consciousness of the act.

Another Ryder Cupper, who has won his share of championships, says his faults are too numerous to mention, but thinks one of his basic faults in the longer shots is the failure to get a good pivot or a good wind-up of the body on the backswing. He says that a good wind-up, or coiling of the power muscles of the body, is essential to produce power and control with the greatest rhythm and timing and with the least strain on the player.

This expert has subconsciously feared losing his balance, and therefore has at times just maintained his position rather than have balance in motion. He most frequently shows this fault in an independent hand, arm, and shoulder swing away from the ball, instead of the more desirable start with the hips and legs. Starting too soon with the arms makes it difficult, if not impossible, to obtain the true wind-up as well as the proper co-ordination of the body, arms, and hands.

When experts run into trouble, they seek the advice of another professional. When you run into faults, do likewise.

DICTIONARY OF GOLF TERMS

To SAVE STROKES IN GOLF, the player should know all about the game and all of its equipment and peculiarities. For this reason, he should know the names of all pieces of equipment, the terms and phrases used to identify conditions, and the various words of golfdom, the free use of which identifies the golfer from the duffer. Hence, the following golf glossary:

Address — Position taken by a player in preparing to start a stroke.

Approach — A stroke played to the green.

Away — The ball farthest from the hole when more than one golfer is playing. Such a ball has priority of turn in playing unless ruled otherwise.

Bent — Grass primarily used on greens and teeing surfaces.

Birdie — Score for a hole played in one stroke under par.

Bogey — Used as an expression for a score of one over par on a hole.

Bogey Competition — A form of stroke competition in which golfers play against a fixed score at each hole of a stipulated round or rounds.

Brassie — A wooden club fitted with a metal sole used on the fairway. It has slightly more loft than the driver.

Bunker — A trap or hazard. That part of a depression where the soil is exposed and filled with sand.

Bye — Unplayed holes after a match has been won.

Casual Water — Temporary accumulation of water which is not recognized as a hazard on the course.

Cleek — A long-faced iron having little loft.

Dead — A ball is said to be dead when it lies so close to the hole that there is no doubt that it will be sunk with the next stroke.

Divot — Sod cut with clubhead after striking ball.

Dormie — A condition existing when a player or side is as many strokes up as there are holes remaining to be played.

Eagle — A score for a hole two strokes under par.

Face — Striking surface of the clubhead.

Fairway — The well-kept portion of terrain between the tee and green, affording the player a favorable lie for the ball.

Fore — A warning to a player that a ball is about to be hit in his direction.

Foursome — A match in which two players play against two, each side playing one ball. This often is confused with a four-ball match, in which four players play.

Green — The putting surface, all ground except hazards within twenty yards of the hole being played as such.

Half Shot — A stroke in which the club is taken back to the vertical position as a maximum of swing.

Halved — When opponents hole out in the same number of strokes.

Hanging lie — A lie in which the ball is resting on a slope which slants toward the hole.

Hazard — Any bunker, water (except "causal water"), ditch, sand, or road obstruction between tee and green.

Head — Part of the club that strikes the ball, as distinguished from the shaft.

Heel — Part of the club at which shaft is fastened to the clubhead.

Hole — Round receptacle in green four and one-half inches in diameter and at least four inches deep. Often metal-lined. Units of play from tee to green. A round consists of eighteen holes or units.

Hole out — Putting the ball into the hole to finish the play for one unit.

Honor – The side or player having priority on a tee. Decided by lot or player or side winning previous hole.

Hook – To hit ball in a curve to the left of the intended line of flight.

Hosel – Hollow part of clubhead socket into which shaft is fitted.

Iron – A club which has a head of steel.

Lie – Manner in which a ball in play is resting. Also refers to angle of clubhead fastened to club.

Links – Term originally applied to a seaside golf course; now, any golf course.

Loft – Angle at which clubface is set from vertical. Used to lift ball into air in flight.

Loose impediment – Any obstruction not fixed or growing. Includes dung, worm casts, mole hills, snow, and ice.

Marker – A scorer, not a referee. Also an object determining forward limits of teeing ground.

Mashie – Usual number 5 iron, loft set at about 40 degrees.

Match – Contest between two or more players or sides.

Match Play – Competition in which results are determined by the number of holes won.

Medal Play – Stroke competition in which results are determined by number of strokes played.

Nassau – A system of scoring: one point allotted for first nine; one point for second nine, and one point for the 18 holes.

Neck – Part of club where shaft joins the head.

Niblick – A heavy, wide iron club with ample degree of loft.

Odd – Indicates a term for the player who has already played one stroke more than his opponent.

Out of Bounds – Ground on which play is prohibited.

Par – Standard score for a hole.

Penalty Stroke – A stroke added to score of a side under certain rules.

Provisional Ball – A ball played after previous ball probably has been lost or is unplayable.

Pull – To hit the ball straight, but to the left of the line.

Push – To hit the ball straight, but to the right of the line. This differs from the slice; a pushed shot is hit straight to the right, and doesn't curve.

Putt – Playing a stroke on the green.

Putter – Club designed for putting. Lie is upright with very little loft.

Rough – Heavy long grass fringing green or fairway, where little effort has been made to condition it for play.

Rub of Green – An expression for a condition arising when a ball in motion is stopped or deflected by an agency outside the match.

Sclaff – To scrape or cut turf with clubhead before impact with ball.

Shaft – Handle of the club.

Shank – To hit the ball with the socket or neck of the club.

Slice – A clockwise spin which causes ball to curve to the right of the intended line.

Sole – Bottom of the clubhead. Act of placing the club on the ground at address.

Spoon – One of the wooden clubs having a thin head, shallow face, and considerable loft.

Square – A match that is even; reference to a stance in which both feet are in a line parallel to the line of flight.

Stance – Position of the feet in stroking.

Stroke – Forward movement of the club made with the intention of striking the ball.

Stroke Play – Same as medal play.

Stymie – When, on the putting green, the opponent's ball lies in line of a player's putt to the hole, providing that ball is not within six inches of the other, and the nearer ball not within six inches of the hole.

Swing – Action by a player in stroking the ball.

Tee – Wooden peg used in starting play from teeing surface.

Teeing Ground – Often called the tee. Starting place for the hole to be played. Indicated in front by two markers. A rectangular space of the depth of two clublengths directly behind the line indicated by the markers.

Threesome — A match in which two players play alternate strokes with one ball opposing a single player. Often confused with a threeball match in which three players play, each playing a ball.

Toe — Forward part of clubhead.

Top — To strike ball above center.

Twosome — Popularly used to describe a "single," in which one player plays against another.

Whiff — Missing the ball entirely.

Waggle — Preliminary action of flexing the wrists, causing the club to swing forward and backward.

ETIQUETTE OF THE GAME OF GOLF

(1) No one should move or talk or stand close to or directly behind the ball or the hole when a player is making a stroke.

(2) The player who has the honour should be allowed to play before his opponent tees his ball.

(3) No player should play until the party in front are out of range.

(4) When the result of a hole has been determined players should immediately leave the putting green.

(5) Players while looking for a lost ball should allow other matches coming up to pass them; they should signal to the players following them to pass, and having given such a signal, they should not continue their play until these players have passed and are out of range.

(6) A player should see that any turf cut or displaced by him is at once replaced and pressed down.

(7) Players should carefully fill up all holes made in a bunker.

(8) Players should see that their caddies do not injure the holes by standing close to them when the ground is soft or in replacing the flagstick.

(9) A player who has incurred a penalty should intimate the fact to his opponent as soon as possible.

(10) Players should at all times play without undue delay.

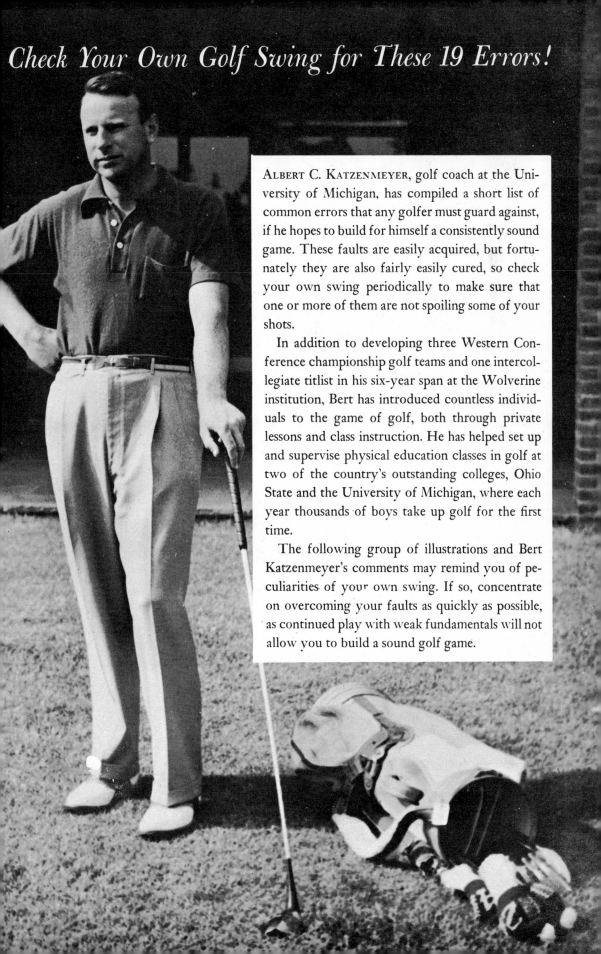

Check Your Own Golf Swing for These 19 Errors!

ALBERT C. KATZENMEYER, golf coach at the University of Michigan, has compiled a short list of common errors that any golfer must guard against, if he hopes to build for himself a consistently sound game. These faults are easily acquired, but fortunately they are also fairly easily cured, so check your own swing periodically to make sure that one or more of them are not spoiling some of your shots.

In addition to developing three Western Conference championship golf teams and one intercollegiate titlist in his six-year span at the Wolverine institution, Bert has introduced countless individuals to the game of golf, both through private lessons and class instruction. He has helped set up and supervise physical education classes in golf at two of the country's outstanding colleges, Ohio State and the University of Michigan, where each year thousands of boys take up golf for the first time.

The following group of illustrations and Bert Katzenmeyer's comments may remind you of peculiarities of your own swing. If so, concentrate on overcoming your faults as quickly as possible, as continued play with weak fundamentals will not allow you to build a sound golf game.

SLICING, OR GETTING POOR DISTANCE? This picture shows the golfer, at address, much too far from the ball. In this "reaching" for the ball most anything can happen, so far as the resulting shot is concerned. Normally, however, loss of distance or a slice will result, because the co-ordination of the hands, arms and body will be very weak.

SLICING TOO OFTEN? It might be because you are carrying your hands much too low at the address, as this golfer is doing, heeling the club head and carrying his hands way down around his knees. This makes it difficult to co-ordinate hands and body in a successful swing.

146

THESE FAULTS ARE EASILY CORRECTED. Here the golfer has been moved up to the ball so that the club is properly soled and centered behind the ball at address. The upper part of his arms are against his chest muscles, thus bringing his hands considerably closer to his body. Also, his knees are slightly flexed so that there is equal distribution of weight between the heels and balls of both feet. The hands have been placed slightly ahead of the club head, directly over the ball, and the player's head is directly over his hands.

ANOTHER CAUSE OF WEAK SHOTS OR SLICES. Here is an exaggerated example of a very common fault, that of disregarding the true line of flight at address. Without realizing it the player may line up considerably to the right of his intended objective. Lining up a shot in this manner will frequently result in loss of distance or a slice.

GET IN THE HABIT OF LINING UP EACH SHOT CORRECTLY. Here, in the correct manner, we find that both the blade of the club and the player's toes are square to the true line of flight. This places his entire body perfectly square to his objective, making possible a successful shot.

IF YOU ARE SLICING, CHECK YOUR GRIP. In this illustration the right hand is too far underneath the club. It's difficult to avoid a slice with such a grip. Check Sam Snead's correct grip in the front of the book and see the difference.

GETTING TOO MANY HOOKS AND SMOTHERED SHOTS? If your grip is similar to this one it might be the explanation. Notice that both hands are placed too far on top of the shaft. Pulled, smothered and hooked golf shots are penalties of this grip.

149

IF YOUR IRON SHOTS GO TOO HIGH OR SLICE, CHECK THIS. Here it should be noted that the hands are slightly behind the club head and the blade of the club is well open to the line of flight. Such faults are normally accompanied by still another, that of placing too much of the player's weight on his right foot.

USE THE CORRECT CLUB FOR EACH DISTANCE. We all know players who brag about getting great distance with their short irons. Most of these golfers do not realize that by playing this way they sacrifice much accuracy and control which could be theirs if they used the proper club, in the manner for which it was designed. This view of a player addressing an eight iron is a good example of this error. For here we find that his hands are way ahead of the ball and that he has toed-in the blade of his club. Thus, he has reduced the loft of his eight iron to that of a five iron. Consequently he will get five iron distance but he will not get eight iron control and accuracy.

DON'T ADDRESS THE BALL IN THIS MANNER. Here the golfer is committing the common fault of addressing the ball with the toe of his club. This sets up a possible shoulder turn at the start of the down swing. Either that, or he will have to move his hands outside the correct downward arc in order to have the blade reach the ball. These errors can easily result in a poor shot, either a pull or a slice.

DO ADDRESS THE BALL IN THIS MANNER. See that the club blade is squarely behind the ball and, in addition, is square to the true line of flight. Thus no change in the path of the hands in the critical area of the down swing need be made.

CHECK YOUR WRIST ACTION AT THE START OF THE SWING. This shows bad wrist action in the away-from-the-ball motion of the hands and arms. As the club head leaves the ball on the back swing the wrists have been cocked at once. This indicates that the club is being controlled by the player's right side and right hand and arm. Such action will normally be followed by the wrists being UNCOCKED too quickly in the down swing, thus robbing the shot of much power.

START YOUR SWING THIS WAY. Here, instead of the club being "picked up" at the start of the back swing, it has been pushed away from the ball, with the left hand and arm thoroughly in control of the action. In this picture, even though the hands have passed well outside the left thigh, there is still little apparent cocking of the wrists. Study again the wonderful pictures in the front part of the book showing Snead's push-away action.

Such action as this practically guarantees a slice. Poor as this swing is, it is quite common. The golfer, although pivoting his hips, has shifted his weight in reverse fashion, and at the top of his back swing his weight is entirely on his left foot.

Topped or sliced shots result from this type of weight shifting. When you end up with your weight on your right foot you look something like this. Such action generally follows the reverse body pivot. At the end of a good golf shot your weight will be on your left foot. Make sure that that is the way you do it.

"SWAYING" RUINS MANY GOLF SHOTS. Here is a clear example of the sway, which is an incorrect transference of weight. For here, through improper body pivot, the player has moved the entire body away from the ball, to the right. The usual result of such weight transference is a sliced shot. It must be remembered that at the top of the back swing there should be a straight line down through the left side, from the chin through the shoulder, the hip, the knee, and the ball.

HERE THE PLAYER HASN'T STAYED DOWN TO THE BALL. The golfer's head should be like the hub of a wheel, remaining relatively constant throughout the swing. In this illustration the player has straightened his body in the back swing, thus allowing his head to come up out of its normal address position. Any one of a number of interesting shots can result from this error, most of them bad, depending upon how agile the player is in returning his head to the proper position at impact.

DON'T DUCK YOUR HEAD OR DROP YOUR SHOULDER. Here, just as the player's hands are entering the hitting zone, and his left side is set for impact, his right shoulder has dropped. His head has thus been brought down lower than it was at address position, and some surprisingly poor results may take place, one of the most common being that of hitting into the turf well behind the ball.

HERE IS THE PLAYER AFTER CORRECTING IMPROPER HEAD MOVEMENT. Notice that the head is in the correct address position and that the straight line through the left side of the body at the top of the swing is very evident. From this position it is easy to start the down swing and go through the critical hitting zone with some chance of producing a successful golf shot.

KEEP YOUR LEFT HAND IN CONTROL. If you allow your left hand to relax at the top of your back swing you will be very lucky to make a good golf shot. This illustration shows that the last three fingers of the left hand, which should be the pressure points for this hand, have been improperly relaxed. This fault will frequently result in loss of control of the club head, thus producing anything but a satisfactory shot.

KEEP YOUR RIGHT ELBOW IN PLACE. This picture illustrates the very common fault of the average golfer of letting his right elbow wander far out of place at the top of the back swing. With the elbow in this position the normal sequel will be a shoulder turn at the start of the down swing, and, consequently, a poor shot. With the elbow out in this position at the top of the back swing it is unlikely that it will drop straight into the right hip line, as it must do for consistently good shot-making.

GRIP YOUR CLUB THIS WAY AT THE TOP OF THE SWING. Here the last three fingers of the left hand have not loosened, and there is little possibility that the club will have to be regripped on the down swing.

Do YOU OVER-SWING, LIKE THIS? The left arm is sharply bent, and the hands are close to the player's right ear, allowing the club shaft to dip far below the horizontal position. When the arms and club get into this position it is quite likely that much control will be lost right at the start of the down swing, and it will be difficult to make consistently good shots.

ANOTHER CAUSE OF WEAK OR SLICED SHOTS. If, as here shown, you uncock your wrists near the beginning of the down swing, you can't help but give up considerable distance which you might otherwise obtain. You will also stand an excellent chance of slicing your shots. When you thus uncock your wrists too soon you may still hit the ball straight, but the hit will not have the power and snap which it might otherwise have, because you will be hitting with nothing but an arm swing. Such an error commonly results from cocking the wrists too quickly as the club head leaves the ball in the address.

SAVE YOUR WRIST POWER FOR THE HITTING ZONE. This shows the correct method of initiating the down swing. The left side does this by a pulling action, and the wrists remain cocked. The right elbow drops into the right hip line and the left arm remains straight.

QUITTING ON YOUR FOLLOW THROUGH CAN BE EXPENSIVE. In this trap shot the golfer has committed two cardinal sins against successful trap play. First, he has failed to finish his swing properly, doing nothing more than chopping down into the sand. Second, he has been too eager to see the result of his explosion, as is shown by the fact that his head has not remained down throughout the action. Failure on the part of a player to finish his shot correctly will often give him the opportunity to try it again, for the chances are that the ball will remain right in the trap.

Outline of your follow-through rite at Heyson. In this frame the
golfer has committed two cardinal sins against successful play: first,
he has failed to finish his swing properly, doing nothing more than
chopping down into the sand. Second, he has kept too much to the
result of his photograph, as is shown by the fact that his head remains
down throughout the stroke. Failure on the part of a player to follow
through freely will give him the opportunity to try again for a
shot that the ball will remain right in the trap.